PASSION TO PROFITS

YOUR GUIDE TO BUILDING A SUCCESSFUL BUSINESS YOU LOVE

BY KIM DAWSON

K.Dawson Company, LLC

For permissions, contact:
media@kdawsonco.com

Visit the author's website: www.kdawsonco.com

Book Format, Illustrations, & Cover Design: Melody Christian, Finicky Designs
Book Editor: Jodi Brandon, Jodi Brandon Editorial
Author Photo: Sandra Costello, Sandra Costello Photography

ISBN-13: 978-1-7337912-0-5

DEDICATION

This book is dedicated to my children, Abriana and Alex, who are at the heart of everything I do, who have taught me how to be the best version of myself, and who inspire me to build a meaningful life while helping others do the same.

ACKNOWLEDGMENTS

I would like to thank those who helped make this book possible.

My editor, Jodi Brandon, who did an amazing job seeing places throughout the book where I could add more useful content, share important stories and information, and simply make the book more robust and impactful for the reader. Jodi helped me to clarify my message and ensure that my thoughts, knowledge, and experiences come through clearly to the reader. Jodi supported me throughout the entire process and I am grateful for her patience, support, and hard work, as well as her efforts in helping me make this book a success.

My book designer, Melody Christian of Finicky Designs, who made both the outside and the inside of the book look beautiful, modern, and easy to read for my audience. Melody worked hard to create a design that matched my brand, and was patient with me as I changed schedules and ideas along the way.

My fellow small business owners and entrepreneurs who help make my business grow and thrive by always being there to support my needs. My graphic designer, Kimberly Osborne of Osborne Designs, who is always there for any project I have going on and is one of the most reliable and professional people I have had the opportunity to work with over the years. My content strategist, Abby Herman of Write Solutions, who understands my brand and purpose and has the talent to craft my message in a way that helps me connect with my audience.

My clients who give me the opportunity to help them grow their businesses, and make me better at growing my own. They give me experience, knowledge, and insight and, without them, I could never do the work that I do. They inspire me to continue my efforts to help others succeed. I appreciate knowing each one of them and their willingness to share with me their aspirations, goals, and successes and allowing me to be a part of their journey.

I would also like to thank my partner and best friend, Dan, who always listens to my day-to-day successes and struggles as an entrepreneur, and who supports and encourages me through everything I do.

Finally, I would like to thank my wonderful children, Abriana and Alex, who inspire me every day to build a business, and a life, that I love.

CONTENTS

INTRODUCTION

If you're like me, an entrepreneur who is also a woman, you will notice there are plenty of places, both online and offline, where women entrepreneurs and business owners congregate. In those places, you will find a lot of motivation, references to mindset and manifestation of success, and other words of encouragement, whether it be reminding others of their value, or reminding oneself.

Feeling supported, encouraged, and motivated, as well as meditating on what you want in life, is powerful stuff, and I recommend it all. In business and in life, your mindset will lead you down the path of success and happiness. Believe in yourself and you will most likely succeed; don't believe in yourself and you probably won't.

However, I see people getting stuck in a place where they are wishing for success, thinking about success, and dreaming about success, without actually taking action to become successful.

I've come to realize the reason for this is that they don't know how to take action, because they lack the education, tools, and strategies needed to do so. This book aims to bring you what so many are lacking: the how-tos of starting, building, and growing your business to whatever place you want it to go.

At times you may find this book challenging. I ask you to dig deep so that you understand the kind of business you really want to have, and how to create a thorough and well-thought-out action plan to make it happen. You will also be doing some number-crunching and calculations, which are necessary if you want to build a successful and profitable business. My hope is that I have presented the material in a way that is easy to follow and understand.

While at times this book will challenge you (because that's how you gain clarity), it is also engaging and fun. Because choosing your life, deciding what you want, when you want it, and actually knowing how you can get it, are awesome.

I have tried to include every major, relevant topic to take you from creating your vision to having a sustainable business model. However, there is no "one-size-fits-all" approach to business. Not everything in this book, then, will apply to every business owner. Take from this book what you find most useful and relevant to your business, and customize it to fit your needs.

Most business owners start their business because of two reasons: They want to work for themselves, and they want to take something they are passionate about and make money doing it. However, the desire to work for oneself and the passion you have to make a living doing what you love are only the first steps. This book will help you create a plan to build a business you are passionate about, that will lead to profitability and long-term success.

The majority of business owners are small business owners, working for themselves and trying to figure out how to survive. My goal is to take you from surviving to thriving by offering you the education and resources you need that are currently lacking in the marketplace.

What makes this book unique compared to other resources out there is that while it contains business concepts that can apply to any size business, it is specifically written for the small business owner, or as I sometimes like to say, the small business entrepreneur or solopreneur. Most business books I have come across, including the vast amount of online resources, come from the perspective that everyone wants to be the next Steve Jobs, or build a massive multi-million-dollar empire. In reality, this isn't true.

Most business owners don't want to build startups, they want to build lifestyle businesses. Lifestyle businesses are businesses that give the owner(s)/founder(s) a certain desired lifestyle and income, without the need to continuously grow bigger. Lifestyle businesses focus on being profitable, while also having time to enjoy life. This book is written with the lifestyle business owner in mind.

If you own a retail business such as a hair salon, a product business such as a boutique skin-care line, or a service business such as an interior designer, I wrote this book for you—to teach you how you can love your work, own your life, and make big bucks doing it.

Whether you're a one-woman show and plan to stay that way, or you can see yourself growing to several employees and running a small but successful seven-figure business, this book can help you build a plan to do it.

This book takes you through the key concepts and components of building your business for profitability and long-term sustainability. It is based upon my experiences as a lifelong entrepreneur, as well as from what I've learned being a strategist, consultant, and mentor to other small business owners working in a variety of industries. Interwoven into the framework are textbook theories on business strategy, marketing, finance, and accounting, blending real-world experience with education-based concepts.

We begin by starting with the foundation for your business, which is about you and your vision. Here we focus on your personal life, including your desired lifestyle, personal goals, values, and dreams, in order to set the stage for your ideal business. Life and business are often intertwined for entrepreneurs, so it is important to make sure you discover ways to connect your desired life to a business that supports it.

We then tackle one of the most challenging, but most results-oriented topics: profitability. You learn how to make your business more scalable and more profitable, and discover various ways to make money in your industry.

Next, we look at fine-tuning your offerings so that you are selling what makes sense for you and your goals, as well as what will bring you the best profit margins. Whether you are selling products or services, you learn effective methods for determining the right prices for what you sell.

Once you know what you are selling, why you are selling it, and that your business can be profitable, it is time to create your brand. The book guides through the process of brand discovery, where you will create a detailed picture of your brand and build it in a way that resonates with you, your business, and your mission.

Your brand will lead to defining your true target market, the audience you are in business to help. You learn how to get very specific when defining your market, and why specificity and creating a niche will help you find quality leads and build your audience.

After creating your brand and identifying your audience, you learn strategies, both online and offline, for connecting with your audience. In this section you discover many different ways to get your audience's attention, how to get them interested in you and what you offer, and the best use of your marketing time and dollars.

Attracting your audience is one thing; closing deals is another. In the chapter on sales and negotiation you learn techniques for selling confidently, authentically, and effectively. You also learn how to qualify your leads, so you don't waste time, and how to follow up after a sales encounter. Many small business owners—in fact, most people—struggle with sales. I discuss the reasons why people struggle and how you can get comfortable with, and even enjoy, sales. You also learn important negotiation tactics to use that will help you and the person you're negotiating with feel like you both come out winners.

Next, we look at the resources you currently have to help you build your business, and what you still need. I show you ways to maximize the value of what you have, how to access what you need, and the most efficient way to use your resources to fuel your path to faster growth and profitability. We discuss building your team, leveraging your network, and how to get help when you lack resources to pay for help.

Now that you've set up all the necessary components of a thriving business, you need to make sure you sustain it. In the chapter on planning for future growth, you learn how to create action plans that will help you achieve your long-term business goals. You also learn how to deal with changes in you business, industry, competition, and market demand over the course of time, in order to use these changes to your advantage.

The final chapter on common obstacles many small business owners face (such as being in a highly competitive industry, having limited resources, few quality leads, or lacking skills necessary for business success) includes various ideas and suggestions to overcome these challenges and rise to success.

Finally, I have included a *Strategic Plan Template* as an appendix you can use to help you build your strategic plan.

So grab a pen, get a notebook, dust off your calculator, and let's get started!

CHAPTER 1

BUILD YOUR FOUNDATION

MY ASSUMPTION AS I WRITE THIS BOOK is that you have already placed the "open" sign on your door, you have launched your business, and you are working hard to build it. However, even if you are still thinking about starting a business, this chapter is just as useful—perhaps even more useful, as it will help you get started on the right foot.

When you launched your business, what did you picture it would look like three, five, or 10 years into the future? Did you even consider this? Or instead, did you decide you wanted to work for yourself, choose an idea that resonated with you, and just start running with it?

Many new business owners feel so overwhelmed by the concept of creating a business and generating revenue, that it is easy to forget to plan for the future. Instead, they live in the moment. I call this being in Reactive Mode. Reactive Mode is when your daily action items revolve around what you need to do immediately in order to deal with what is happening to you, or around you.

For example, this could include responding to emails and phone calls, posting on social media, signing up for local networking events, and reaching out and introducing yourself to potential customers. While these tasks will help you get a new customer, discover a new opportunity, or keep your business alive, you are not actually taking *action* on the process of building your business. You are simply *reacting* to what happens when you own a business.

Staying in Reactive Mode might sustain you for a short length of time, but you will most likely not grow your business to the place you'd like it to be, and you certainly won't see it reach its potential. You need to get clear on your overall vision for your company. This means not looking at what you need to do today (find new customers, build a social presence, and pay the bills), but looking at where you want to see your business in the future.

You start with the broad questions, such as:

- ❑ Do you want to have a local business or go national, or even international?
- ❑ Will your business rely on in-person transactions, or will it be online?
- ❑ Do you want to be a one-person show or do you want employees? If so, how many?
- ❑ What about partners? Investors?
- ❑ Do you want to grow your business for the life of it, or are you looking to build and sell?
- ❑ Do you see yourself owning a business that generates $250,000 in gross revenue per year, or is it a $1 million, $5 million, or $50 million?

Granted, you might not know all of the answers to these questions, as they will likely evolve over time as you learn and grow your business, but you should have some general idea of where you are heading and what you hope to accomplish over the life of your business.

But before you make too many decisions about the business you wish to build, there is an important exercise I'd like you to do. This exercise will help you answer both the broad and detailed questions about what kind of business you want to create. It will help you define your business vision.

This exercise consists of three components: defining your ideal life, identifying who you're trying to help, and determining what financial success looks like to you.

DEFINE YOUR IDEAL LIFE

For the first component, **you need to do a little soul searching and get clear on what your vision is for *your life*.** Your business is much more than a job that pays you or some add-on to your life and existence. Your business is a part of who you are, and it is woven into your life and identity. You don't want to treat it like a separate entity, mutually exclusive from everything else.

Your business will determine your overall lifestyle. It will affect your relationships with your family, your children, significant others, and yourself. It will affect how you spend your time, with whom you spend that time, where you live, what you own, your hobbies, where you travel, what your retirement years will look like—and this list goes on. It will even affect your values and beliefs.

Determine what you want *for your life* before your decide on what you want for your business. Even if you are several years into your business, do this exercise. You might be surprised at how much you learn about yourself, and the direction your life and business are taking as you move forward. You will also be able to see if that direction is what it should be.

The next several pages include questions to help you gain clarity around your ideal life. Use this exercise as a blueprint for creating the life you desire. **Answer the questions not from your current state, but from where you'd like to be.** For example, to answer "Where do I live?" visualize yourself living in your ideal life, not where you live right now. Of course, they may be (and hopefully are!) one in the same.

I suggest using a notebook for this exercise, one you will keep for a while and revisit from time to time. Perhaps add to the notebook, over time, various business ideas you have, plans, and goals. Remember: These answers may change over time, which will cause your ideas, plans, and goals to change, as well.

MY IDEAL LIFE EXERCISE

1. Where do I live?

   a. I live in (name the town/city/state or country).

   b. I've chosen this place because _____.

2. What is my relationship status?

   a. I am happily: (circle one) married without children, married with children, single and independent, single with significant other, single with children, divorced, other.

3. What type of community do I live in?

   a. I live in a community that is: (circle one) rural/suburban/urban.

   b. I've chosen this community because _____.

   c. This lifestyle makes it easy to _____ and difficult to _____.

   Example: Living in an urban city makes it easier to manage my household (i.e., no need to mow a lawn or maintain a house every weekend, thus freeing up my time). It is more difficult to travel (i.e., may be difficult to own and use a car, therefore may need to rely on public transit and stay close to home, which could limit who I can work with and where I can travel to for work).

4. What are the **top three** most important aspects of my life?

   Example: The three most important aspects of my life are my family, my health, and my financial independence.

5. What activities do I absolutely need time for each week?

6. Where do I prefer to spend the majority of my time? (Circle your top choice, then place an asterisk next to any others that are applicable as places you also enjoy spending time.)

a. Home

b. Office, mostly working in solitude

c. Office, mostly working with others

d. Retail/shops, consumer-oriented businesses

e. Social networking venues/public events

f. Fitness and wellness facilities

g. Outdoors/in nature

h. Driving and/or traveling

i. A combination of several listed above

7. When do I prefer to work? (Circle one.)

a. Weekdays, 9–5

b. Weekdays, any time of day

c. Weekdays, early mornings and early afternoons

d. Weekdays, afternoons and evenings

e. Weekends

f. Both weekdays and weekends, as long as I can pick and choose my hours

8. How many hours per week do I wish to work? (Circle one. Be reasonable here, but also choose what makes you happy.)

a. 50+ hours per week (I'm a workaholic and I love it!)

b. 40–50 hours per week (I like to work full-time, but need one or two days off per week.)

c. 30–40 hours per week (I like to work most days of the week, but need time for self-care, hobbies, and spending time with family/friends.)

d. 20–30 hours per week (I have many responsibilities aside from my business, and work needs to be part-time in order for me to feel balanced and productive.)

e. Fewer than 20 hours per week (I have other priorities that are more important than my work. I'm looking to spend more time on those aspects of my life and less time working.)

9. If you chose answer c, d, or e in #8, what activities do you spend your time on when not working?

10. Three things* I want to have in my life are _____.

**I try not to use the word* things, *as it isn't very clear or descriptive, but in this case I'm referring to anything that you really want to obtain, earn, buy, have, or accomplish in life. They can be things you already have or things you plan to get in the future.*

My answer: I would like a beach house, long-term sustainable income, and the freedom in my schedule to spend a lot of time with my children.

11. If money were not a concern, and you had five* years left to live, how would you spend those five years?

**Why five?* You've heard people say, "If today was your last day, what would you do?" I don't like this question because it won't help you gain any clarity. If you only had one day left to live, you would never choose to go to work, go to the gym, or do anything productive. You would most likely be focused on spending time with your loved ones, and perhaps eating a lot of cheeseburgers and ice cream, but not much else. By giving you five years, it invites you to think about what you would choose to do with your life if you knew time was limited (which it is, but we tend to not think about that) to make you happy and give you purpose. You'll also be more likely to think about setting goals and working toward achieving them, but also think about balancing that work with other aspects of your life that bring you joy.

When you look at your answers above, do you notice any trends, and specifically how does your ideal life compare to what you are living now, and your future or current business? For example, if you wrote that you want to spend a lot of time with your family, travel the world, and work four days a week from home, but your business requires you to work away from home and work 60+ hours a week for the life of the business, then you might have some reevaluating to do.

Use this exercise to reflect on what you need and want to be happy in life, and make sure it aligns with your business model and aspirations.

IDENTIFY WHO YOU HELP AND WHY

After you have identified what makes you happy and the kind of life you wish to lead, it is time to look at how you want to help others. You can't be in business for the sole purpose of self-pleasure. In other words, if you decide to open a restaurant only because you love to cook, you won't succeed in business. No one will pay you to do what you love to do if there isn't anything in it for them. However, if you want to create meals and a dining experience that others will enjoy, now you have a chance at success.

No business can truly exist long term without a mission or a purpose for helping and serving others. After all, why would anyone give you money if they don't get something in return? Aside from the financial transaction that takes place, if you currently own a business, or are thinking of starting one, hopefully you have some motivation for helping others.

When you first came up with your business idea, who were you hoping to help? Why do you want to help them? What are you hoping the results of your help will be? Is your desire to help enough to motivate you to spend time, money, and risk on building a business around this idea?

The answers to these questions will help you craft your mission statement. Many companies spend a lot of time creating the perfect mission statement. However, don't get bogged down into trying to make your mission statement super trendy or full of marketing buzzwords. The point is to get a clear message across, which is difficult to do when you get too creative with your statement.

A mission statement should tell the world WHY you are in business, WHAT you do, HOW you do it, WHO are you in business to help, and what RESULTS or VALUE you bring. Some companies make the mistake of making their mission statements so short, they don't include these important components. You don't want them to be too long either, though. Try to state your who, what, why, and how in the most succinct and easy-to-understand manner as possible.

While mission statements are important for conveying your message to others, I would argue that they serve *you* more than your market. Sitting down and writing a proper mission statement gives you the opportunity to clarify and define the foundation and purpose of your business. Once you've done this, everything else you do becomes so much easier. Deciding who your market is, as well as where and how to market to them, determining the best methods for generating income, and discovering the ideal candidates for helping you grow your company all will be easier with a well-written mission statement.

Spend some time thinking about the questions above and complete the following:

I WANT TO HELP (who)____

BY OFFERING (what)____

BECAUSE THIS WILL GIVE THEM
(results)____.

I WILL BE ABLE TO PROVIDE THIS BY
(how)____.

Next, try to come up with a few example mission statements you can use for your business in the space below.

Here are a few examples of company mission statements:

PATAGONIA - *"Build the best product, cause no unnecessary harm, use business to inspire and implement solutions to the environmental crisis."* - from Patagonia's website, www.patagonia.com/company-info.html

JETBLUE - *"JetBlue's mission is to inspire humanity – both in the air and on the ground. We are committed to giving back in meaningful ways in the communities we serve and to inspire others to do the same."* - from JetBlue's website, www.jetblue.com/jetblue-for-good/

HONEST TEA - *"Honest Tea seeks to create and promote great-tasting, healthy, organic beverages. We strive to grow our business with the same honesty and integrity we use to craft our recipes, with sustainability and great taste for all."* - from Honest Tea's website, www.honesttea.com/about-us/our-mission/

If you already have a mission statement, ask yourself if your business reflects your answers. In other words, are you helping those you wish to help, and are you effective at doing so? Finally, do they value your offerings?

DETERMINE YOUR DEFINITION OF FINANCIAL SUCCESS

In my experience, most people—not just business owners—fail to choose how much money they want to make in order to feel successful. You may be thinking, "What does she mean by *choose?* Since when can we choose how much money we make?"

If you're thinking this, my answer would be "Since forever!" For example, if you went to college, you had to choose your major. When you made this decision, you knew that you could major in finance, accounting, medicine, or law, and perhaps someday have a six-figure salary; or you could choose social work or elementary education and be lucky enough to make $50K a year. You could also have chosen a major like art or music, and be lucky to have a job at all!

The point is, the decisions you make determine not only the salary you earn, but how much money you can make in your business. The key is to first start by not thinking about what you *do,* but thinking about how much money you *need* in order to accomplish your goals. These goals are not just goals for your business, but goals for your ideal life, as you identified in the My Ideal Life Exercise.

For example, if one of your life goals is to own a vacation home, travel to 30+ countries, or send all four of your children to college, then you need to determine how much money you need to do it. Financial success is defined differently, depending on the individual, and there is no right or wrong. There is only what is right for *you* and whether you are creating a financial path to support what you want.

Someone who is an artist may define financial success as making enough money to support themselves so they can spend their time doing what they love: creating art! This might mean making $60,000 per year, renting a small apartment, and having enough money to travel, with no frills, a few times a year for inspiration. They might live in a city and have no need or want for a car, nor a desire to have a closet full of fancy clothes. But they may want enough money for high-quality art supplies.

Another person may define financial success as having so much money, they never need to worry about money! Perhaps they want a beach house, a summer car and a winter car, multiple vacations a year at five-star resorts, and the ability to go shopping whenever they feel like it. For this lifestyle, one may need to earn $500,000 per year or more.

The point is, you need to decide how much money you need to live your ideal life, and then build your business plan around that. Here is an example scenario:

Jesse is a freelance copywriter living in Arizona who works remotely and makes about $35,000 per year. However, she dreams of moving to San Francisco and owning her own condo near the water. This lifestyle will require her to make close to $100,000 per year, much higher than what she currently makes.

Jesse has identified her ideal life and how much money she needs to make in order for that to happen. However, she sees a challenge when she realizes that her current income situation is much different from where she needs to be. Rather than throwing in the towel and saying it's impossible, Jesse needs to figure out how she can take what she loves to do (write copy for advertising and marketing) and turn it into a business in which she can generate $100,000 each year in personal income.

If I were advising Jesse, I might present the following possibilities to consider:

1. **Target higher-paying clientele.**

   Currently her market is small business owners who have no employees and are in need of inexpensive (affordable) copywriting. However, Jesse is a very talented copywriter and could be valuable to larger small businesses that are more profitable, such as companies with 25+ employees or more than $5 million in annual revenue.

If Jesse rebranded her business to target these higher-paying, larger, and more profitable companies, her contract fees could be much higher.

2. **Create a niche market.**

    Jesse currently works within a variety of industries. In other words, if the phone rings, she takes the client. However, Jesse could carve out a niche area for her business, making herself an expert copywriter within a certain field, such as technology, finance, or health and fitness. By creating a specialty niche, she will be able to create more demand for her services and be able to charge higher rates.

3. **Build an agency.**

    Jesse can build an agency—not just around copywriting, but an advertising agency, a social media and branding agency, or a small business services agency. The idea would be to come up with a few related services that companies need, and offer these services a la carte or as packaged products for higher-revenue clientele.

    One benefit to this idea is that companies would be willing to work with such an agency on a consistent basis, making revenue projections easier and more reliable. Jesse could build a staff of business professionals who can complement one another and be able to provide many valued services.

    As she would be building a company, rather than a small business of one, Jesse would be able to enter a new, higher revenue bracket for her business.

These are just a few ideas, but you get the picture. You can take anything you are passionate about and find ways to convert it into a revenue-generating business. Doing so simply requires that you be open-minded and explore new ideas. You also need to have an understanding that certain revenue models (a fancy term for ways you make money) are naturally more profitable than others.

I'm saving my big spiel about profits for later in the book. For now let's talk about how it relates to your vision of financial success and your path to choosing the right revenue model.

Look back at your answers to the My Ideal Life Exercise. To connect these details to your financial needs, let's simplify it to how much money you need to make each year in order to live your ideal life.

Considering your desired lifestyle, activities, assets, and place to live, how much do you need to earn each year to pay for it all? Before deciding too quickly, choose an amount that you *really want,* not what you think is realistic. If you want to travel four times a year, own two homes, and be able to donate 10% of your income to charity and put another 10% away for retirement, then figure out what that number is and write it down!

For the following exercise, once again get your notebook and write down your expenses based on your ideal life so you know how much money you need to make in order to cover your expenses.

The purpose of this book is not personal finances, but let's make a general estimation of what that number would be for you. You can fill this out monthly or annually, whichever is easier for you. Of course if you fill this out using your monthly expenses, don't forget to multiply by 12 to get your annual amount.

NOTE: This is meant to be filled out using your ideal numbers, not your current numbers.

YOUR EXPENSES

Home/mortgage $____________________

Personal taxes $____________________

Home expenses *(utilities, heat, phone, etc.)* $____________________

Food $____________________

Clothing $____________________

Insurance *(auto, home, life, etc.)* $____________________

Automobile $____________________

Education $____________________

Travel $____________________

Personal expenses *(hair, nails, personal care)* $____________________

Medical $____________________

Household expenses *(supplies, maintenance, repairs, etc.)*

$ ____

Other *(shopping, entertainment, childcare, and any other expenses)*

$ ____

YOUR TOTAL EXPENSES $____________

Phew! Now you know how much personal income you need to earn in order to live the life you desire. In the next section, we'll look at whether or not your business can support your lifestyle goals, and if not, how you can make that happen.

CONNECT YOUR VISION TO A VIABLE BUSINESS

So here's the big question: *Does your current business* ***have the potential*** *to generate this amount of revenue for you?*

Let's look at an example to help you answer this question. Suppose you are a wellness coach and fitness instructor. You work as a subcontractor in various facilities, teaching classes and working with clients. Your business expenses are fairly low because you don't have your own facility. Marketing yourself is difficult because you are in a highly competitive industry, and it's tough to get the word out. Your available time is limited, and the amount you can charge for classes and clients needs to stay within your industry averages. You sustain yourself with a few consistent clients, and you teach five to seven classes per week. Here is what a simple income statement (also called a profit & loss statement, or P&L) might look like for you.

Note: Don't panic if you don't know what the terms gross *and* net *mean. For now just know that* gross *means the amount you earn* **before** *taking into account your expenses. It's typically the amount you charge your customers.* Net *is how much money you make* **after** *subtracting your expenses.*

YOUR DESIRED INCOME EXAMPLE

SALES (per week)

Classes (7 per week x $100 per class)..$700

Client sessions (10 per week x $65 per session)..........................$650

Total Weekly *Gross* Sales..$1,350

EXPENSES (per week; annual fees divided by 52 weeks)

Travel (gas, parking fees, etc)..$50

Insurance...$10

Certification/CEUs/professional license..$5

Equipment/supplies..$10
(equipment for clients/classes)

Professional services..$10
(accountant, legal)

Software subscriptions $15
(online scheduling, contact management, etc.)

Conferences $10

Networking/marketing $10

Total Weekly Expenses $120

Total Weekly Net Profit $1,230

If this were your situation, you would be earning approximately $59,040 per year, before taxes ($1,230 x 48 weeks; I like to assume four weeks out of the year people don't work due to vacations, illness, travel, children, etc.).

Let's say the *ideal* personal income you chose in Your Desired Income Exercise is $120,000 per year. Your current business puts you halfway of where you want to be. Ask yourself is doubling your income is possible considering your occupation.

Can you simply double what you are doing now—take on 20 clients and teach 14 classes a week? I highly doubt it—unless you want to be completely exhausted all of the time and work 60 hours a week. You have to ask yourself, then, if there is another way to do what you currently do, and make the income goals you have set out for yourself. Or are you on a dead-end path and need to re-evaluate the nature of your business?

Just because your current business is unable to generate your ideal income, as in this example, that doesn't mean it's time to throw in the towel. Not at all! You need to look at all of the different possible directions you could take in your current business, or in your current industry/skill/trade, to get in line with your personal goals, just as I demonstrated earlier in the chapter with Jesse, our Arizona copywriter.

CREATE YOUR INCOME STATEMENT EXERCISE

Create a simple income statement specific for your business. Maybe you already have one, which would be fabulous! As a consultant, I know too often how many small business owners don't keep track of their numbers, so here is a template just in case you're part of that majority.

To figure out your net profit, subtract expenses from gross sales. To calculate your gross sales total, list your services and/or products and how much you charge for each, then add them up to get your total gross sales amount. You can use a weekly, monthly, or annual number, whichever is easier for you.

To calculate your expenses, list your expenses and how much you pay for each, then total them to get your total expenses for the week/month/year. Use the same calculation (weekly, monthly, or annually) for both sales and expenses.

Common expenses include:

Salaries

Payroll taxes

Employee benefits

Independent contractors

Consultants, lawyers, accountants, and other business professionals

Rent/lease payments

Advertising/promotion

Website maintenance

Office expenses

Utilities

Insurance

Bank fees/interest

Travel

Meals and entertainment (for clients/customers)

Office supplies

Software subscriptions

SALES

(Product/service 1) ....$ ________________

(Product/service 2) ....$ ________________

(Product/service 3) ....$ ________________

TOTAL GROSS SALES........$ ________________

EXPENSES: Write down the total in the space below.

EXPENSES

(Expense 1).............................$ ________________

(Expense 2).............................$ ________________

(Expense 3).............................$ ________________

TOTAL EXPENSES .... $ ________________

TOTAL NET PROFIT (*Gross sales – Expenses*) $ ________________

NOTE: Did you include your personal income in your salaries expense, or do you not take a salary and, instead, draw from your net profit? There are different factors to consider when choosing one method over the other (salary vs. owner's draw), such as type of business entity you have (S-Corp, C-Corp, LLC, Schedule C/sole proprietor, or partnership) and whether or not your business is profitable. Because of tax implications, it is best to consult with your CPA or tax accountant to determine which method, as well as which business entity, is best for you. For this exercise, just make sure you account for your income somewhere.

How does this income statement compare to Your Ideal Income Exercise? Did you include your ideal income in either your salaries expense or as a draw from your net profit? If so, can you still make an overall profit for your business? If not, can you realistically see your business generating enough money to support your desired lifestyle? If it's not there right now (which is probably why you bought this book), start thinking about ways you can get it there.

In summary, you've created the vision of your ideal life, identified who you are trying to help, and stated the amount of money you need to make in order to make it all happen.

Bringing together all of the exercises in this chapter, complete the following:

- ❑ Write a one-paragraph summary of your ideal life (based on the My Ideal Life Exercise).
- ❑ State the group of people you help—your target market.
- ❑ Identify how much money you need to earn each year to afford the lifestyle you want.

CHAPTER 2

BUILD A PROFITABLE BUSINESS

YOUR MONEY-MAKING MODEL

THE OUTLINE FOR THIS BOOK began as a manual I created for a workshop I offered. It was a one-day workshop and I broke the content into four sections. The last section was all about revenue. I was afraid if I started talking about numbers too early in the day, I would lose people's interest, and they wouldn't want to continue! I've been working with business owners long enough to know that most of them, especially small business owners, don't want to be bothered with math, accounting, bookkeeping, or talking about "the numbers side" of their business. So I put all the fun stuff in the beginning of the manual, including branding, marketing, and designing your ideal client, and waited until the very end of the day to talk money.

However, this generated two unfavorable results. First, I ran out of time to cover all the details I wanted and left people hanging in the middle of their financial plan, an area where everyone probably needed the most clarity and guidance. Second, I realized that it doesn't make sense to talk customers, branding, marketing, and more without first having your financial road map. You need to make sure your revenue model is a viable one before you start taking the show on the road, so to speak. Imagine how you'd feel if I spent an entire book helping you get clear on your market, brand, and sales strategies, just for to get to the very end and find out the whole idea isn't going to work! You'd be pretty peeved.

Therefore, here at the near-beginning of the book, I'm going to ask you to start crunching numbers and thinking all about money: how much money you can potentially earn, how much you're going to need to run your business, and how you're going to make it happen.

I also want to add that it's okay to be overwhelmed by the numbers side of your business, and it's okay if you get through the chapter and still feel confused. I don't expect you to simply "get" all of this stuff in a half hour. You may need to go back to it, again and again, until it starts to make sense. Be patient with it, try to focus on understanding the overall ideas and concepts first, and then later on work out the details if that is most helpful to you.

Technically, this section is about something called a revenue model. But as I looked at this term, I realized it made the book feeling more like a textbook and less like a "take charge and make it happen" kind of book. "Money-making" sounds better, right?

The model can be defined as the structure or foundation of how you make money, which includes your different sources of income (revenue streams) and how profitable each source is for your business (profit margins).

Revenue streams are the different sources of your income, which can include products you sell, services you provide, fees you charge, rent you charge. Most businesses have multiple revenue streams, and my advice is that most businesses *should.*

Net profit margin refers to how much money you earn from what you sell after taking into account all of your business costs (net profit), and comparing it to the amount you make before considering your expenses. In other words, net profit margin is how much bang you get for your buck. It gives you an idea of whether a product or service is really worth selling. You calculate it by taking your net profit and dividing it by your gross revenue, and representing it as a percentage.

Example: Suppose you sell Product A for $25, and it costs you $15 to make. Your net profit is $10 and your profit margin would be 40% .

Net profit / gross revenue = $10/$25 = 0.4 = 40%

This means that when you sell Product A, 40% of the price you sell it for is profit, and the other 60% is your cost to make it.

Note: There are three types of profit margins: gross, operating, and net. For now, we'll focus on net because it represents your overall ability to be profitable.

UNDERSTAND PROFITABILITY

Why am I spending so much time talking about profit margins? Because as a business owner, it is crucial that whenever you sell *anything*—a service or a product, or even fees—you look at your profit margins to determine if it's worth it to sell it. Understanding and knowing your profit margins will give you insight into what revenue streams are worth exploring, what you should try to sell more of, and what you should perhaps stop selling.

EXAMPLE:
Imagine you sell three products.

Product A:
Sales price = $25
Cost to make = $15
Net profit = $10
Profit margin = 40%

Product B:
Sales price = $45
Cost to make = $20
Net profit = $25
Profit margin = 55.5%

Product C:
Sales price = $30
Cost to make = $10
Net profit = $20
Profit margin = 66.6%

A novice might look at the sales price only and tell themselves, "Hey, I can make more money if I sell more Product B, since it is my most expensive item for sale." But when you compare the profit margin of each product, you will see that while Product B is your highest-priced item, you actually earn a greater profit margin from Product C.

This doesn't mean that you stop selling Product B. In fact, a 55.5% profit margin is good. You also make a greater amount of total revenue from Product B; net profit is $25 for each item sold.

This example just gives you an idea of which of your products are most profitable compared to their respective costs.

Let's look at another example.

EXAMPLE:

This time, we'll compare just two products.

Product A:
Sales price = $50
Cost to make = $40
Net profit = $10
Profit margin = 20%

Product B:
Sales price = $45
Cost to make = $20
Net profit = $25
Profit margin = 55.5%

Notice that Product A and B are selling for close to the same price—$50 vs. $45—but Product A has only a 20% profit margin and Product B has a profit margin of almost three times that, at 55.5%. In this case, you might want to consider phasing out Product A and focusing on selling more of Product B.

> **If this is confusing for you, don't panic. Just understand the basic concept—you want to make as much money as possible compared to the cost—and apply this principle to making decisions around what you should and shouldn't be selling.**

Now, if you're a service-based business, and you don't have direct manufacturing costs associated with products, does any of this matter?

Yes, it does. Here's why: The most common cost of doing business for the service professional is your time. Instead of looking at product cost, compare time (your true cost) to revenue, and figure out which services are worth keeping and which aren't. Also note that net profit and net profit margins look at *all* of your business expenses, both manufacturing as well as the costs associated with running your business. (This includes that long list of expenses from Chapter 1.)

EXAMPLE:

Suppose you offer two services for your clients.

Service A: Sales price is $100, time it takes you to perform service is 2 hours. Profit per hour is $50.

Service B: Sales price is $250, time it takes you to perform is 2 hours. Profit per hour is $125.

Comparing these two services, Service A gives you profitability of $50 per hour and Service B gives you profitability of $125 per hour. Clearly you should be focusing on selling Service B, and not Service A.

In real life, though, your business may require that you offer both. As a hair stylist, for example, you have to offer both color and cut, but color may be more profitable. If this is the case, as it usually is, the idea is to push sales of Service B over Service A.

In the example of the hair stylist, you could do this by setting a maximum amount of time each day for haircuts, so that the majority of your day is designated for color.

Another reason to keep both services is that sometimes Service A helps sell Service B. A new client may hire you for a simple haircut initially, then, if they like you, book a color service in the future. Or you may be able to upsell products and services at the time of purchase. For example, suppose a client wants a haircut, but you upsell them on getting Balayage highlights, or purchasing haircare products such as conditioning hair serum or thickening lotion.

As you will see in the example list of Complementary Ideas for Service Providers (see page 43), you can benefit from selling multiple products and/or services, such as upselling mastermind clients to purchase one-on-one coaching, or clients looking for business card design can be upsold to full portfolio design.

The take-home point in all of this is to understand that there are many options available to you for making money. Your job is to choose the options that make the *most* money.

Whether you are creating a business plan for a brand-new business or have been in business for a while and want to be more profitable, you need to take the time to evaluate or reevaluate your offerings for maximum profitability.

The next section helps you do just that.

But first, one more point regarding profitability: It's important to understand that generating sales, regardless of how large, doesn't make you profitable. The difference between what you are bringing in (your sales) and what is going back out (your expenses) is what matters. In other words, your business could be generating $5 million a year in sales, but if you have $6 million going out, you're not profitable, and you're losing money.

This may seem self-explanatory, but you'd be surprised how many business owners I meet who don't take the time to run their numbers and mistakenly think they are making money simply because they are selling. I see this often with service professionals who give clients flat-rate fees, and don't figure out how much time it actually takes to get the job done. They may charge a client $500 for a job that took 20 hours, and after they calculate not only their time, but all of their business expenses, they are actually *losing* money. They are *paying* to work. (Yes, really.) Make sure this isn't you!

PROFIT MARGIN / PROFITABILITY EXERCISE

Plug in your own numbers to determine how profitable your products or services are for your business.

Product Business

Item: ____________________

Sales price (per item)	$____________
Cost to make (per item)	$____________
Net profit per item *(sales price – cost to make)*	$____________
Profit margin per item *(net profit / sales price)*	____%

Example:

Item: Facial Cleanser

Sales price (per item)	$ 25
Cost to make (per item)	$ 10
Net profit per item *(sales price – cost to make)*	$ 15
Profit margin per item *(net profit / sales price)*	40%

Service Business

Service ______________________

Sales price (per service) $____

Hours worked performing service (per service) ______

Net profit per service *(sales price / hours worked)* $______ (per hour)

Example:

Service: Corporate Event Planning

Sales price (per event)	$ 10,000
Hours worked performing service (per event)	80
Net profit per item *(sales price / hours worked)*	$ 125 / hour

NOTE: These are very simplified examples for illustrative purposes, only. In order to have accurate numbers you must take into account actual costs of running your business. For example, while you may charge $10,000 for corporate event planning, and the time you spend on this particular event is 80 hours, we have not accounted for the costs of running your business, such as what you spend on office space, phone/internet, marketing, taxes, and so on.

However, this exercise does give you your earned hourly rate for the job. Assuming you follow the formula for pricing your services explained in the next chapter, this hourly rate can be compared to the amount you need to earn in order to cover your costs, provide you with your desired salary, and give you extra for savings and growth.

SCALABILITY

What is scalability? Think of scalability as the difference between eating 2 ounces of lettuce and 2 ounces of cheese. You're eating the same amount of each food, but the cheese gives you much more energy than the lettuce. A scalable business model gives you greater income potential than a non-scalable model that is much less profitable.

Some businesses are fully scalable in nature, such as a product-based business; other businesses are not scalable, such as a service-based business. Scalable business models show an exponential growth of sales, while non-scalable business models have linear growth, with a maximum number of sales possible.

With a linear model, the amount of money you earn is proportional to the amount of time you put in. For example, if you charge $100 per hour for your services and you work 10 hours, you will make $1,000. If you double the amount of time to 20 hours, you will also double the amount of income to $2,000. On a graph, it would look like this:

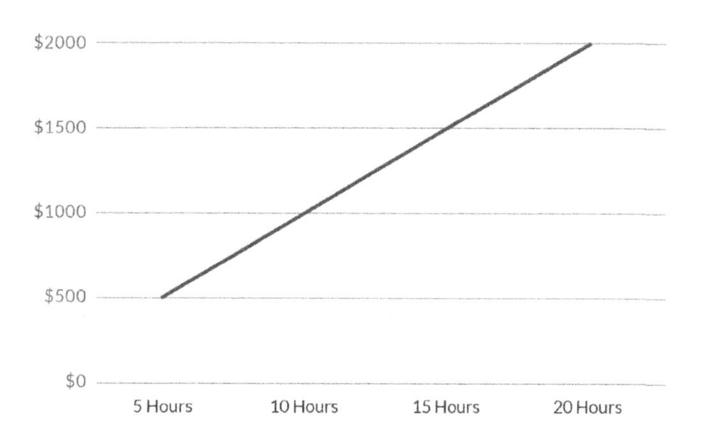

Clearly, you max out at a certain point, as your time is limited, which creates a maximum amount of potential income. For example, if you are a graphic designer, you spend your time working on client design projects, and you most likely bill them based on this time (though I suggest you stop doing this; more on that in a moment). You only have time to work on so many projects per week, so if you bill based on time or project, there is a limit to your weekly revenue. You also need to decide how many hours you have available to work per week, and that may be 30 hours for some, but as much as 60 hours for others.

Using this in an example, a graphic designer may charge $125 per hour and have 30 hours per week available for *billable hours,* with an additional 10–15 hours per week for marketing and administrative work.. This would give you a total weekly revenue of $125 × 30 = $3,750. Unless you add a scalable component to your revenue model, this is the most you will be able to earn.

A scalable model isn't about sales being proportional to time. Rather, it is about exponential growth of sales over a period of time. If you were selling a product, it could look like this:

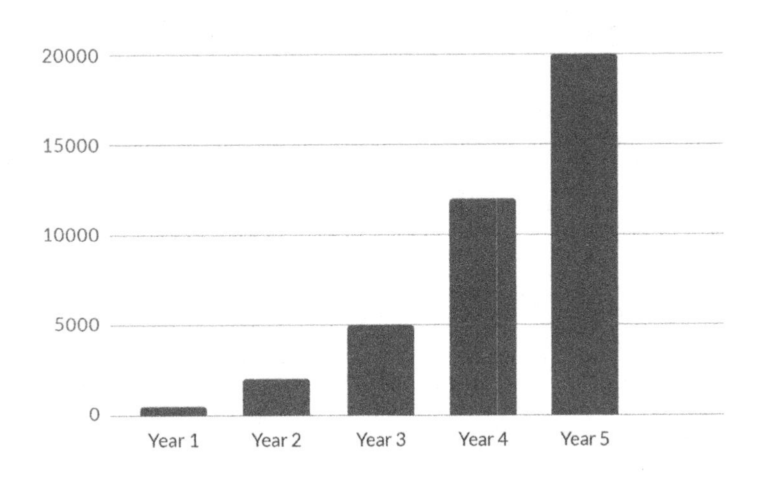

Notice the exponential projection from Year 1 to Year 5. Equating this to dollars, you could sell 100 units in Year 1, earning $10,000 in sales, and by Year 5 you could be selling 20,000 units, generating $2 million in sales. With this type of business model, you can continue on an upward projection, making the income potential much higher than in a linear, non-scalable model.

If you are in a product-based business, part of your sales projections and goals will involve setting realistic expectations of units sold per year, and will include seeing an exponential increase in sales and profits (at least, that is the plan). However, a service-based business can incorporate scalability *into* their business by selling products that complement their service, or by franchising if they have a business that would make sense to franchise. For example, if you were a personal chef, you could write a cookbook or sell an online course that teaches people how to cook.

Here are a few ideas for service-based businesses to incorporate scalability:

1. Hire others who perform services that complement yours, or who can perform the same services as you but have no interest in being business owners themselves. Build a team of employees, with your job being to oversee and manage the operations and direction of the business.

2. Think about products you can create that complement your services (or even replace them). This can include physical products people purchase or products that are not physical in nature, such as membership programs, classes, and online subscriptions.

Complementary Product/Service Ideas for Service Providers

Hair Stylist	Haircare product Beauty classes and workshops (online or in-person)
Personal Chef	Food products (gourmet food line) Group cooking classes (cooking school) Online instructional videos/programs

Accountant	Small business services company Bookkeeping service with multiple bookkeepers on staff
Photographer	Subscription-based stock photos website Online photography retailer
Business Coach	Online classes Conference Membership program Group training
Personal Stylist	Online personal styling software Membership-based community In-person workshops
Career Coach	Online employment agency
Writer	Writing courses Online membership program for writers
Fitness Instructor	Certification program for a particular fitness method, training program, or system

The chart gives just a few examples for various professions, but I encourage you to look at your own profession and industry, do some research online, and discover ways to use your talents and passions to build a scalable business model.

If you're a product-based business, you can make your business more profitable and growth-oriented when you expand your product line, increase your profit margins by reducing your costs, increase areas of distribution by partnering with similar companies offering complementary products, or make your products more exclusive, sold at a higher price.

Take some time to generate different ideas for making your business more scalable or more profitable.

CREATE YOUR MONEY-MAKING MODEL

Now that we've talked about the concepts of profitability and scalability, it is time to look at creating your own money-making model (aka revenue plan). To create yours, you need the following components:

- A list of products/services you provide
- The costs of making your products/providing your services
- The prices you charge your customers
- Your sales projections (how much quantity you will sell, and in what time frame you will sell it)

The next several chapters will help you develop each of these components.

CHAPTER 3

WHAT DO YOU SELL?

WHILE WRITING THIS BOOK, I struggled with deciding which would be better: to have you define your offerings, and then build your audience and brand from that, ***or*** to have you define your audience and brand first, then decide what to offer.

I came to the conclusion that there is no right or wrong way to approach this; I could make an argument for either. Some companies start with an idea for a product, usually because it is lacking in the marketplace and they recognize the need for it, while others want to help a particular group of people and then work to discover what product or service would be helpful to them.

I decided to make this chapter more of a broad overview of what you sell, focused on concepts more than details, and to introduce it before pricing, branding, and marketing. Read this chapter to absorb the ideas, but you can wait on getting into the specifics until later in the book if you prefer.

You may already have products and/or services that you sell, but business owners should always review what they offer and ask themselves if their offerings are still marketable, relevant, and profitable. Therefore, even if you've been in business for several years, I encourage you to go through this chapter with fresh eyes and make sure that your offerings are what and where they should be.

When you're designing your business model (aka how you're going to make money), you often ask yourself this question: What exactly am I going to sell? This process is different for everybody.

Some people start with the thought that they want to own their own business, but they aren't sure what they want their business to be; they just know they want to be self-employed. They begin to seek out ideas, sometimes based on their personal interests, and sometimes based on recognizing a need and wanting to fill the void.

For others it starts with an interest in something, and then deciding that they could make a business out of their interest. Whichever the case may be, you need to figure out what you are going to sell, and what value it brings to others. Where business owners fall short is that they think from their own interest and perspective, but don't always consider whether what they are selling is valuable to anyone else. (By value, I mean that others are willing to pay for it.)

Your personal interest should guide you to the point of knowing what industry to work in, such as knowing you want to work in fashion and not healthcare. Allowing yourself to be open-minded can help you generate profit-worthy business ideas that satisfy both your need to create what you love and what your customers want to buy.

Here's an example of how you can apply this thinking toward making your business more satisfying and profitable. Suppose you live in New York City and you've always dreamed of opening a pizza shop where customers make their own pizza. You love this idea because you don't see anyone else doing it in your neighborhood, and you know it would be fun. You imagine people choosing your make-your-own-pizza place as an activity for the whole family and a place to enjoy good food and community.

However, most families are busy during the week and would likely only visit your business on the weekends. While it may be fun at first, after a few visits, your customers will probably get bored with the novelty and realize it is quicker, cheaper, and easier to just grab a slice on their way to the park. Space will also be very limited, and realistically, how many families can be prepping pizza at the same time? Finally, with the high price of rent for retail space in Manhattan, you'll probably never make ends meet trying to survive on a business that's only busy two days a week, with the need to continuously generate new customers.

So how can we tweak this to make it a more sustainable and profitable business?

First, we go back to the question: What do you sell?

Your initial response may be "I sell pizzas you can make yourself." In fact, this is not what you sell. You are selling an experience. When you sit back and think about this dream, what excites you is not selling pizza; it's creating a place where people can connect with their family and friends while cooking one of America's favorite foods. You want to help people enjoy the simplicity of loved ones coming together and sharing an easy-to-make, homemade meal. Once you realize this, it opens up ideas for various "products" you can offer to create the experience you desire for the group you want to help.

Instead of selling make-your-own pizza, perhaps it would make more sense to create a *specialty store with cooking classes*. You can sell homemade foods that people love, alongside a classroom where people can learn how to cook delicious, easy-to-make meals. The menus can change each week, and you can offer theme classes and private parties as well. Classes can be more than just learning skills. You could offer a "cook and sip"–style class, where there are wine and socializing, for example.

Why is this a better idea?

- ❑ This model doesn't just appeal to families, but to adults who might be interested in taking classes as well. You could perhaps offer family classes during weekend days, and adult classes on both weekday and weekend evenings. Or maybe you create a niche market, geared toward discerning adults. It could be a popular place for date nights, small parties, and special occasions.

- ❑ City dwellers love to be able to get good, fresh food easily. Remember: New York isn't the 'burbs, where you can hop in your car and load your SUV up with Costco boxes and eight grocery bags. Having a small storefront with appealing everyday-yet-gourmet foods will be a big hit in a city neighborhood.

- ❑ This model will create repeat business. The store portion will have the same people stopping by every week. And while the cooking classes are more of a novelty, because there are different meals being prepared and taught each week, there is a reason for people to keep coming back and trying new recipes. In the case of the pizza shop, it's always going to be pizza. Nothing new to explore.

The takeaway here is that if you want to build a successful, profitable, and sustainable business, you need to first look at what you really want to sell (in this case, the experience of community combined with homemade food and cooking), and then think of product or service ideas that will help you maximize sales and use, minimize obstacles, and have repeat customers instead of constantly seeking new ones.

CHAPTER 4

PRICE YOUR SERVICES FOR PROFIT

MANY SERVICE-BASED ENTREPRENEURS I meet undercharge for their services, then wonder why they are working full-time and not making any money! One of the leading causes of this is that most people don't know *how* to price their services, so they choose numbers that are similar to competitors or that just "sound good." I'm going to teach you how to be more scientific about your prices and discover what you *should* be charging.

There are several methods you could use, but the one I use with my clients looks at your business expenses and your desired salary, and adds an additional amount to cover the costs of unexpected expenses, to build savings, and to prepare for future growth. Most service-based business owners forget to charge for their expenses, let alone tack on extra for savings and growth. But think of it this way: If you were an employee, you would be paid a salary, a portion of which would go to taxes and retirement, and your employer would be also paying taxes on your salary, *plus* they would be paying for an enormous amount of overhead. When you work for yourself, you need to compensate for these costs.

Many business owners equate what they charge their customers or clients with what they would be paid if they were working for someone else, and that doesn't work. You're comparing apples to oranges. You need to charge enough to cover your desired salary, taxes, expenses, retirement, savings, and extra for future growth. You won't be able to grow your business if you are just scraping by. You need to build savings to afford growth in the future, such as moving into bigger space, investing in new products, or hiring staff.

Let's start crunching the numbers to see how you can apply this to your own business.

1. Calculate your total annual expenses. This should include your rent, insurance, office supplies, advertising costs, software subscriptions, utilities, travel, business taxes, and anything else you regularly spend money on each month or year. Add all of these expenses to get to one total annual cost. I suggest using the numbers you calculated in Chapter 2.

   For this example, I will use $30,000.

2. State your total annual desired salary. This is how much you want to make each year, before taxes are taken out. For example, if you desire a salary of $125,000 as if you were an employee, then pick this number.

3. Finally, add a third number. This number represents all of the extras we mentioned. You calculate this number by taking the sum of your business expenses and your desired salary, and dividing by 2. Here is an example:

If your business expenses are $30,000 per year and your desired salary is $125,000 per year, the sum of these two is $155,000. $155,000 divided by 2 equals $77,500. Therefore your third number is $77,500.

Here's what this looks like:

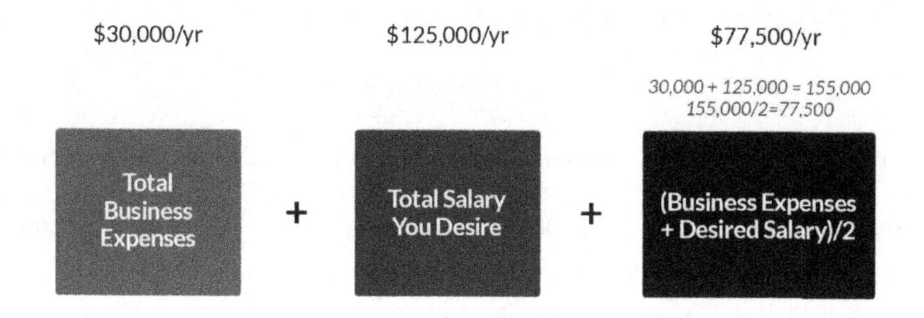

Next, add the three numbers to get your grand total.

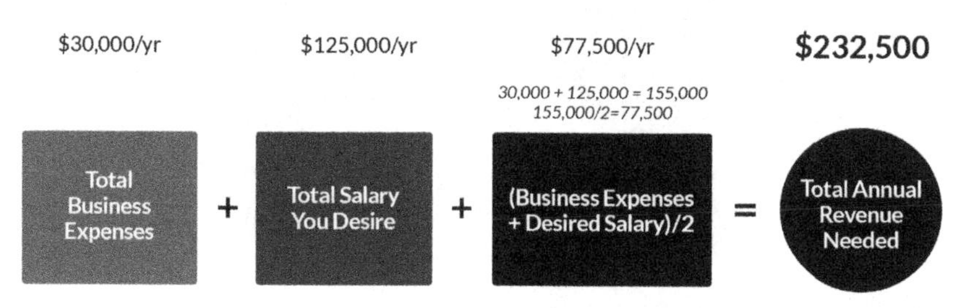

In this example, if you are a service-based professional, your business expenses are $30,000 per year, you want to earn $125,000 per year, and you want to build savings for future growth (and retirement!), you need to be generating $232,500 per year.

Now that you have determined your total annual revenue needed (again, calculate this using your own numbers), the next step is to equate this back to your pricing. In order to do this, you need to ask yourself how many client hours (billable hours) you can work each year. There are two considerations in computing this number:

1. You probably don't want to work more than 20 billable hours per week. The remaining hours will be needed for non-billable time (marketing, networking, administrative, etc.). It's a standard estimate to say that half of your week will be billable and the other half not billable.

2. You want to allow for time away from work (e.g. vacations, travel to conferences, and children requiring care during school breaks and holidays).

> In other words, you didn't go into business for yourself so you can have 10 vacation days a year. You want flexibility, so account for it in your pricing. (I would pick four vacation weeks per year, if it were me.)

So how many client hours (billable hours) per year?

20 hours per week × 48 weeks in a year = 960 hours available for billing clients

If you need to generate $232,500 per year in revenue, and you can generate this revenue for 960 hours per year, then divide your annual revenue by your available billable hours to get your hourly rate.

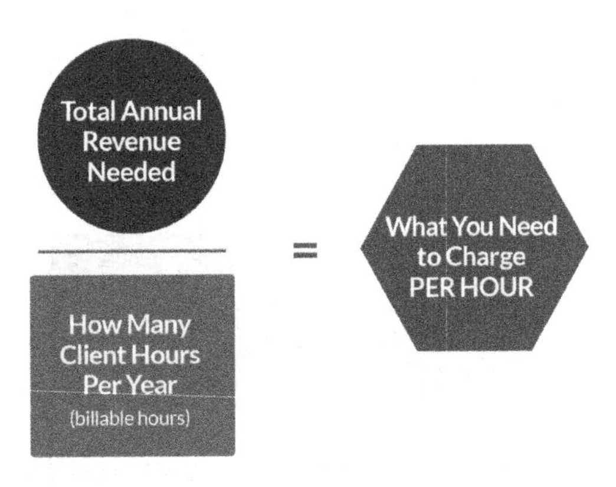

Here's what this looks like using our example numbers:

If this were you, your billable hourly rate would be $243 per hour. Once you have determined your hourly billable rate, it will become much easier to price your services and feel confident that you will be profitable—and financially better prepared for the future of your business and your personal wealth.

On the following pages, you can calculate your own billable rate based on your current expenses and desired salary.

ANNUAL REVENUE NEEDED

YOUR CALCULATIONS

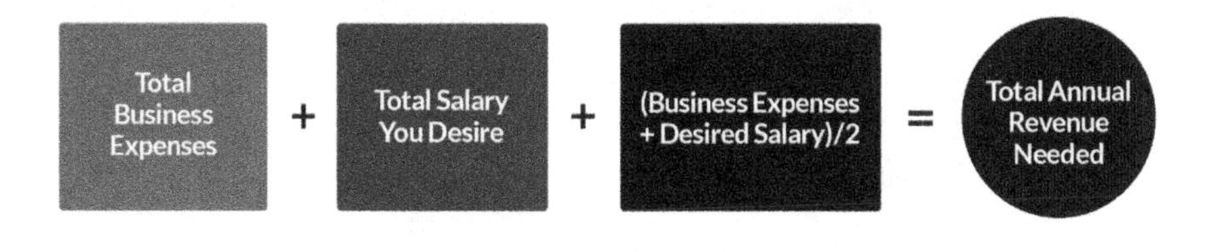

TOTAL ANNUAL REVENUE NEEDED:

Sample business expenses include:

- Salaries
- Payroll taxes and benefits
- Consultants
- Rent/lease
- Advertising/promotion/website
- Office expenses
- Utilities
- Insurance

- Bank fees and interest
- Professional services (accountants, attorneys, graphic designers, etc.)
- Travel
- Supplies
- Software subscriptions

HOURLY RATE
YOUR CALCULATIONS

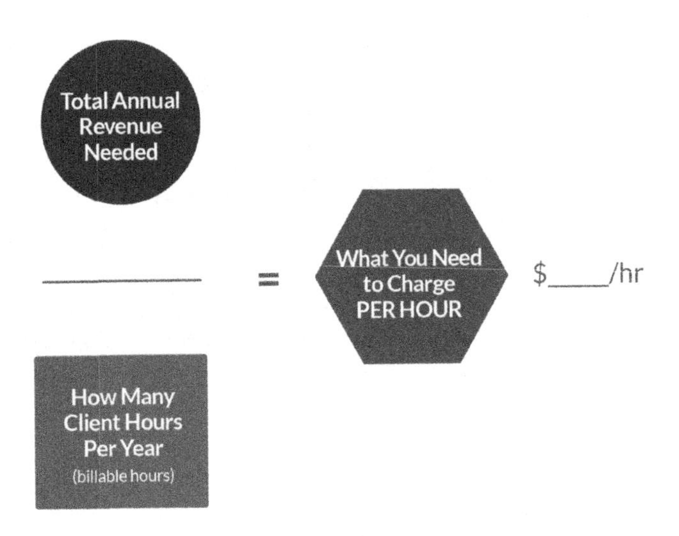

If you're like most of my service-based clients, you compute this number and then realize you are charging too little for your services. You may also be thinking, especially if there is a large discrepancy between what you are currently charging and what you should be charging, "How am I going to get my current clients to start paying me this much more?!" I will validate your concern and let you know it isn't an easy situation to be in, but it *is* a common situation. Just remember: You're not in business to lose money, so you can't continue to charge your current rates if you ever expect to be successful and reach your goals.

RAISING YOUR PRICES

The question then becomes: If you are going to increase your rates with your current clients, what is the best approach? The first step, even before contacting your current clients, is to ensure that all of your current offerings are updated. Each service you offer should have a title, description, and updated price. For example, a graphic designer may have a list of services such as logo design, brand identity portfolio, business card design, website design, and so forth, and each would have a description of the work involved along with the respective package price or hourly rate for each.

Once you have updated your list of services, email all of your clients notifying them of your price increases. Depending on your business, you could choose to write a personal email to each client, or you could send one email to all of your clients. I recommend the latter.

Why? Because in my opinion, it looks more professional and is digested easier. We have all received letters from vendors letting us know of price increases at one point or another. When you receive one of these letters, it is usually formal, giving a brief explanation that rates are going up for "xyz" reasons (usually cost increases or yearly inflation) and concluding with a thank you for being a valued customer. You may not like the news, but you understand, realize it's part of business, and move on.

However, if a vendor reached out to you personally to tell you their rates have gone up, you might still be fine with it, but you may also wonder if these new rates really apply to everyone (or are they just trying to get more out of you?), and you may also be more apt to respond in protest.

What should the letter include? Assuming you are only increasing prices, and not changing services or packages offered, you could focus on the following:

- ❑ How you/your services are bringing **value** to your clients
- ❑ How your services can, and will, continue to help them
- ❑ How you are committed to providing excellent quality, value, and service

You should also include the need for increased pricing to cover the costs of running your business as well as let them know that you welcome any questions they may have.

This covers the content of the letter, but the form and structure matter just as much. When I was in graduate school I learned about a teaching technique that can be used when presenting constructive criticism. It works like this: You start by saying something positive, then offer your criticism, then conclude with something positive. I have adopted this method for presenting bad or unfavorable news as well, and have found it to be extremely helpful in business, and in life.

Here is a sample letter I wrote for a client to send to their clients after deciding to increase their prices.

Hello!

We are so excited to be a part of one of the most memorable days of your life, and are committed to making it everything you envision it to be. Our goal is to take care of as much of the back-end work as possible so that you can truly get lost in the moment.

We are always focused on giving our clients the best experience (and service!) as possible and it is necessary for us to evaluate our offerings each year to ensure we are doing just that. In the coming weeks, we will be sharing with you some exciting news about new products and services we will be offering to help make your big day as easy and simple as possible!

Additionally, we wanted to notify you of our updated pricing and payment policies for 2018. As of January 1, 2018, our payment structure is as follows:

[New rates and payment policies]

If you are a current 2018 client, we will be billing you according to our new 2018 payment policies going forward. If you have any questions about our updated policy, please reach out.

We are so grateful for all of our wonderful clients, and look forward to helping each of you experience one of the best days of your life.

Thank you,

As you can see from this letter, it begins with something positive, focusing on how they are committed to giving their clients the best experience possible. Then they focus on exciting, upcoming new offerings and how these will help their clients. They briefly mention they are updating pricing and policies as part of their yearly business evaluation and state the new rates and policies. They conclude with their gratitude for their clients and offer to answer any questions.

Will you lose clients when you increase your prices? Most likely, but if you provide a worthy service, you won't lose more than a few. Can you afford to lose some of your clients? I will answer that question with another question: Can you afford *not* to? Can you afford to go on charging less than you need to survive? No, you cannot.

Have faith that if you set your prices accurately, you will build a clientele that will pay those prices, you will attract higher-paying clients, and your business will thrive in the long run.

We'll delve further into these concepts in the branding chapter, but here are a few key points to remember:

- ❑ Don't be afraid of your prices, as long as they are founded on reason.
- ❑ Your prices are a part of your brand. They must be accurate and authentic to your message and mission.
- ❑ Focus on your niche, and align your pricing with that niche.

YOUR PRICES SPEAK VOLUMES!

STAY MOTIVATED

We've discussed many reasons to price accurately, such as earning a living, while also covering the costs of running your business, saving money, and preparing for future growth. We've also discussed how pricing can affect your brand and reputation within your market. One more important reason to price right is to keep you motivated!

Remember: It was your initial passion that led you to start your own business. That passion motivated you to either quit your day job, take out a loan, or work long hours to get your business off the ground. While it's not practical to expect that each and every day you'll wake up with a smile on your face anxious to get to work, as all business owners have ups and downs, you should look forward to work most of the time if you're going to stay motivated enough to keep working at growing your business.

Motivation is essential to keeping any business alive. When you work hard but barely turn a profit, you wind up feeling resentful about your business and will most likely not be motivated enough to provide your clients with a high level of service. Your business will suffer, and you might eventually build a poor reputation, which will cause you to have a more difficult time charging what you need in the future.

If you are happy with your prices, however, you will feel better about your business and the work you do, and you'll stay motivated to continue to work, build your business, and provide excellent customer service. Pricing accurately will not only keep you motivated, but will communicate to your market the quality and value you provide.

Pricing your services so that you are profitable, are able to save and plan for future growth, and stay motivated is key to making your business thrive. When determining your prices, it is also important to consider your desired lifestyle, another passion you had when starting your business. You went to work for yourself so that someone else wouldn't dictate your work hours and lifestyle. Make sure you set your prices support the number of hours you want to work.

If it makes sense for you to work 40 hours a week, and 20 of those hours are non-billable, as we discussed previously, price based on working 20 billable hours per week.

Remember: You have every right to charge based on the value you provide, charge for actual costs to run your business, enjoy the lifestyle you want, and create a profitable and long-lasting company.

CHAPTER 5

PRICE YOUR PRODUCTS FOR PROFIT

SIMILAR TO PRICING SERVICES, pricing products involves looking at your costs, such as your business expenses and the cost of making your products, as well as your desired profitability. Aside from business costs and desired profitability, your prices will also be determined by what you can realistically expect to sell with regard to quantity and market demand. For example, if you are selling a product that is highly in demand but difficult to produce in large quantities, your prices will be higher. In contrast, if your product is readily available by multiple competitors that can easily mass produce the product, your prices will be lower.

Let's first look at the simple numbers of it all. In order to do this, you need to understand one concept that can make pricing products a little tricky, in comparison to pricing services.

With services, you have your business expenses and your time. You can easily figure out, as we did in Chapter 4, how much time you have available to work, and how much money you need to make for that time in order to cover your costs and additional desired profit. With products, however, it isn't as simple. Most companies sell multiple products, and various quantities of each, making it more difficult for the small business owner to tie overall business costs to sales price.

The difficulty is in the complexity of allocating costs to individual products. For example, say you spend $5,000 per month on rent, and you manufacture three items: one at $50, another at $150, and another at $500. If you sell 10 of the first item, five of the second, and two of the third, how do you figure out the amount of rent that should be associated with the cost of selling each product? You can do it, but it is a lot of work that most small business owners don't want to be bothered with.

I am fairly certain I just made your head spin. The good news is that you don't need to worry about all of that. I'm going to give you a simple method for determining the right prices for your products, without having to go nuts doing advanced cost accounting.

PRODUCT COSTS

We're going to start by just looking at your products and the costs of making them (also known as COGM, or cost of goods manufactured), without looking at your other business costs for the time being. Make a list of your products and include how much they cost to make (called your *direct* costs). Here's an example for a manufacturer of a skincare line:

Product	Cost to Make (COGM)
#1 Moisturizer	$12
#2 Eye Cream	$9
#3 Wrinkle Serum	$15

For each business, your COGM is different, depending on how you manufacture your products. You may outsource and have another company make your products for you, which charges you a flat rate per item (you simply pay them for manufacturing the product), or you may produce in-house. If you are unsure what your COGM is, it usually consists of the following: raw materials, labor, direct manufacturing, and overhead costs. It does *not* include costs outside of directly making your product, such as marketing costs, administrative costs, or rent on your office space.

In our example, your COGM would be the ingredients that go into the skincare products, the packaging, the labor of those manufacturing the products, and any expenses related to paying for the facility they are manufactured in, or, if not in-house, what you pay the manufacturer.

As a small business owner, you are most likely either making your products in your small office/kitchen/industrial space facility or you are outsourcing. If this is the case, and you want to be really accurate on direct facility costs, then look at your overall overhead cost and figure out what percentage is used for manufacturing your products.

For example, suppose you are manufacturing the skincare products listed earlier in your 2,000-square-foot (SF) office/industrial space. Your office takes up 500 SF; the remaining 1,500 SF are used for making and assembling the products. Now suppose your rent is $5,000 per month and your utilities are $1,400 per month. Because you are using 75% of your space for manufacturing (1,500 SF/2,000 SF), you can say that 75% of your overhead costs of rent and utilities are used for manufacturing. In this example, it would equate to $4,800 being a direct cost of manufacturing your products ([$5,000 (rent) + $1,400 (utilities) = $6,400] × 75% = $4,800).

If we assume that the cost of materials is $4, the cost of labor is $2, and you make 800 moisturizers per month, your COGM might look something like this:

Product: Moisturizer

Cost of raw materials (per unit): $4
Cost of labor (per unit): $2

Cost of overhead (per unit): $6 ($4,800/800)
Monthly overhead costs: $4,800
Units produced each month: 800

Total COGM = $12 per unit

If you are thinking that pricing services is much easier than pricing products (it is), have no fear! I promise this will start coming together and you will be able to implement it in your own business pricing.

The example is meant to give you an idea of how you can accurately determine your costs of making your products. Once you have done this using your own numbers, it should begin to make sense and you will see that it is easier than you think. In summary, here is what you need to know:

- ❑ The cost of your raw materials: *the ingredients or products that go into making your product*
- ❑ The costs of packaging your products, *such as bottles, boxes, and labels*
- ❑ The cost of labor for those *making* your products: *the people actually producing or assembling your products*
- ❑ The overhead costs associated with making your products, *such as rent and utilities of the space where manufacturing and assembly takes place* (This will be easiest to calculate by looking at the monthly costs and dividing by units made per month.)

Again, for some of you these costs are determined by the manufacturer you outsource to, and therefore your COGM is simply what you pay to them, per unit. It is also worth noting that shipping costs for your products are *not* a part of COGM. COGM are only the costs that go into making the products. Shipping costs come after the product is already made.

One final question you might have is "Well, I sell multiple products, so how do I determine the cost of each if they all share the same manufacturing facility?" Good question.

If you look at the list above, the first three items are directly related to each item, regardless of how many items you make or how many items you have. The tricky piece is really the fourth item in the list: overhead costs (which is actually really easy once I show you how to calculate it!).

The easiest way to approach this is to do what we already did: compute your monthly overhead costs and divide by the number of units you produce each month. It doesn't really matter what the variety is, or how many different products you sell. Here's an example using our skincare line:

Overhead costs (monthly):

Rent - $5,000

Utilities - $1,400

Total overhead costs = $6,400

Products manufactured (monthly units produced):

Moisturizer - 800

Eye cream - 600

Wrinkle serum - 200

Total units produced = 1,600

Overhead cost per unit= $6,400/1,600 = $4 per unit

Simple as that! Each unit carries the same overhead cost per unit, but the *percentage* of the total overhead cost is different. In other words, if you make 800 moisturizers, 600 eye creams, and 200 wrinkle serums in a month, each one carries $4 of the total monthly overhead cost, but the moisturizers make up 50% of the overhead costs (800 out of 1,600 units), the eye creams make up 37.5%, and the wrinkle serum makes up 12.5%.

Putting this all together, here is the cost of manufacturing the wrinkle serum (again, using example numbers for materials, packaging, and labor):

Product: Wrinkle Serum	
a. Raw Materials	$4
b. Packaging	$2
c. Labor	$5
d. Overhead	$4
Total Cost	$15

<u>COGM vs. COGS</u>

You now know what COGM is, but you are probably more familiar with the term COGS, *or* cost of goods sold. *COGM is the cost associated with manufactured products, regardless of whether or not they are sold. COGS is specific to the manufactured items that have been sold. It is most often used on the income statement in order to recognize the manufacturing expense associated with the items you have sold and are claiming as a source of income.*

WHAT'S YOUR PRICE POINT?

Now that you know more than you ever wanted to know about pricing products, we get to the fun part: determining how much you should sell them for to make a mighty profit!

In order to choose the right prices for your products, we will look at two things:

1. Your desired profit margins
2. What the market is willing to pay

YOUR DESIRED PROFIT MARGINS

I've mentioned it a few times, but remember: *You* get to *choose* your profits. I just love that! Yes, when companies work on pricing for products, they start by choosing a desired profit margin. These margins are chosen, within reason, but can also have great flexibility depending on your industry and what the market is willing to pay.

More details on that to come, but for now, let me ask: What is your desired profit margin? Before you answer, let me address that typically different kinds of products will each bear slightly different margins. As I talked about in Chapter 2, your job is to look at what you currently offer and what the profit margins are, and focus your efforts on the products that give you the best rate of return.

At this point we are not looking at what you already have and comparing, but we are going back to the beginning and *choosing.*

How do you choose a profit margin? Start by looking at your desired income (as you did with pricing your services) and move backward. For example, suppose your skincare company (we'll stick with this scenario) consists of you, two full-time employees, and two independent contractors. You sell online and through boutique retailers, you're in your fifth year of business, and you're currently generating $500,000 in profit.

You are planning to get into more retail stores, expand into international markets, and grow your product line over the next five years. In order to have the investment capital needed for growth, as well as the money to pay for more employees and contractors, your revenue goal for the upcoming year is $750,000, followed by $1 million for the next year, and so on.

Your sales and product costs currently look like this:

All Products:

- ❑ 1,600 units manufactured (and sold) each month = 19,200 units for the year
- ❑ Each unit's cost to make (COGM or COGS), on average = $12 per unit [($12 + $9 + $15)/3]
- ❑ Total cost of goods sold for year = 19,200 units × $12 per unit = **$230,400**

Your current cost of manufacturing/COGM/COGS is $230,400, based on selling a total of 1,600 units per month at an average cost of $12 per unit. Your revenue, or total gross sales, is $500,000. Let's assume your other business expenses (salaries, office rent, insurance, marketing, administrative, etc.) total $250,000 per year.

Your income statement would look like this:

Total Sales	$500,000
– COGS	$230,400
Gross Profit	$269,600
– Expenses	$250,000
Net Profit	$ 19,600

This means that you are currently profiting, after all expenses are paid, **$19,600 per year,** and your **profit margins are a mere 3.92%** (Net Profit/Total Sales, or $19,600/$500,000).

Clearly, you are not where you want to be, and in this example, you are probably charging twice the cost of making your products (i.e., a unit of moisturizer that costs $12 to make is being sold for approximately $24), and this is far too low of a cost to fuel your business forward. The additional $12 that you've tacked on to the cost of making the moisturizer is simply going to cover the costs of salaries, office rent, and the other business expenses, but you're not really very profitable.

Remember from the beginning of this section that the first step in determining prices is determining or choosing your profit margin, and step two is seeing what the market will bear. In this case, you will choose a desired profit margin, but you must also recognize that you are not selling enough product to cover your costs, but with sales growth *and* better pricing, you will be more apt to be profitable.

Continuing on, let's say you decide that you would like your profit margins at 20% instead of 3.92%. How does the backward method work?

We look at our income statement again and leave a few fields blank. We know that our desired net profit should be 20% of our total gross sales. We also know that we are currently selling 1,600 units per month (19,200 per year), that cost $12 per unit, and our annual business costs, aside from COGS, total $250,000.

Total Sales	$	
– COGS	$230,400	
Gross Profit	$	
– Expenses	$250,000	
Net Profit	$	(Net Profit/Total Sales = 20%)

The easiest way to calculate this is on a per–unit basis, then fill in the previous afterward.

You know that your COGS is $12 per unit, but we have not yet calculated the amount per unit associated with running your business. If you sell 19,200 units per year, and your business expenses are $250,000 per year, that means that each unit sold carries an additional business cost of approximately $13 per unit ($250,000/19,200). Therefore the total expenses, COGS + Business Costs = $12 + $13 = $25.

So your true cost per unit is $25 (average of the three). Adding in a 20% profit margin will give you a sales price of $31.25 ($25/.8 or 80%).

In summary, if you sell 19,200 units per year, at a sales price of $31.25 per unit, and all other costs being equal, your total sales for the year will be $600,000, and your approximate net profit margin will be 20%.

Your income statement will now look like this:

Total Sales	**$600,000**
– COGS	$230,400
Gross Profit	**$369,600**
– Expenses	$250,000
Net Profit	**$119,600** (Net Profit/Total Sales = **19.9%**)

If you are starting to feel like you are in over your head, don't panic. This is tough stuff! I don't expect you to understand all, or even most, of this right now. Come back to this material and reread it, go through it again and again, until it starts to click. The goal here is to get you thinking about pricing your products so that you can cover your costs and be profitable, as well as lead you to a place of growth and prosperity. The more accurate your pricing, the better chance you have of being successful at this.

A few important notes before we move on. First, in reality, your quantities will fluctuate while your business costs may not, so this example isn't 100% accurate. For instance, whether or not you sell 19,200 units in a year or 22,000 in a year, there is a good chance that your business costs (salaries and rent) will stay the same. It's simply to help you understand the basic principles.

Another important note is to look at the original example, in which the net profit was $19,600 and a profit margin of 3%. This is the equivalent of almost breaking even. Your break-even point (BE point) occurs when your income is the same as your total expenses, and you "break even." I used this example so that the process would be easier to follow, and the numbers would be believable and easier to work with.

If I started out with a situation in which you were losing money, it would have been harder to go from a loss, where your expenses aren't in line with your sales, and then adding a desired profit margin on top of it. In reality, this may be what you need to do, but I wanted to keep our example as simple as possible.

You should know what your break-even point is, at any point in your business. Usually it is equated to either units you need to sell or dollars you need to bring in to cover your costs. It will help guide you in making smart business decisions.

Suppose all of your business costs equal $450,000 per year, and this is based on selling 18,000 units per year at $30 per unit. You could say that your break-even point is either $450,000, or 18,000 units, or $30 a unit. If you know this, you know that if your sales go below $450,000 for the year you are going to lose money and be "in the red." This will also be the case if you sell less than 18,000 units, or you drop your prices below $30 per unit. Use your BE point to monitor the state of your business.

The phrase in the red *refers to a financial loss (whereas saying you are "in the black" means you're profitable). It comes from using an accounting paper ledger where positive money numbers were traditionally written with black ink and negative numbers were written in red ink.*

Over time, all of this will make more sense to you, you'll learn as you go, and you'll realize why it matters. In the meantime, I'll simplify it so you have something to work with today.

1. How much money have you spent making your products in the past year?
2. What's the cost of running your business (this includes salaries, rent, utilities, marketing, software, office expenses, legal, accounting, etc.) over the past year?

3. How many units have you sold?
4. What's your break-even point for each unit?
5. How much profit do you want to make per unit?
6. What will you sell your product for?
7. What will be your net profit for the year?

Example Answers:

1. $50,000
2. $150,000
3. 5,000 units
4. Cost = $200,000 ($50,000 + $150,000)
   / 5,000 units
   = $40 per unit is the break-even price
5. $10 per unit profit
6. $50 ($40 + $10)
7. $10 profit per unit × 5000 units sold = $ 50,000 profit

WHAT THE MARKET IS WILLING TO PAY

Now for the second piece (not done quite yet!): what the market will be willing to pay. We just looked at determining the right price for your products, based on your costs and desired profitability. We did not yet discuss whether or not your market will pay those prices. After all, if I want to make a 75% profit margin, why can't I just do that?!?

Honestly, you *may* be able to do that—if the market will pay it. For example, I have a hard time believing that a $1,000 handbag has the same profit margin as a $25 handbag. Luxury brands can go after higher profit margins, because their market is willing to pay them. It all comes down to what you make, what industry you are in, and what your market values.

I'm a firm believer that you can choose your prices, as long as you provide value to your market, there is a market for what you sell, and you have a solid business plan to back it up. People are willing to pay $1,000 per night in hotels, spend $200,000 on a wedding, and buy $10,000 watches. You can name your price if the product, value, and market are just right.

This all depends on the brand you create. You can build your brand to highly exclusive products, therefore charging high prices; you can go middle of the road, and charge mid-range prices; or you can focus on creating an economy brand that appeals to the masses, with economy prices to go with it. You can't, however, build an economy brand and charge luxury prices.

We discuss competition in Chapter 12, but I want to mention now how competition should, and shouldn't, affect your pricing (since so many choose their pricing based on what their competitors charge).

First, while it is good to know what your competitors charge, don't let them dictate your prices unless you are selling the *exact same* item. (You aren't.) There will almost always be something that differentiates you and allows you to justify your own prices. We've already discussed the most important factors in your pricing: knowing the cost of making your products and charging at least that, plus more so you can profit. Your competitors will have different costs and different profit margins.

That being said, if your product is similar to your competitors, you can't be totally off the mark. You must provide the level of value, quality, and service that are expected at your chosen price point. For example, if you are running a nice, middle-of-the-road hotel, and your competitors are all charging anywhere from $125 to $250 per night, you're off the mark if you decide to charge $500 per night. However, if there is something that makes you just a little bit better than the rest, you could theoretically go up to $300 and justify it. What your market is willing to pay will be dependent on the brand you create. People will pay $1,000 a night to stay at a Four Seasons, but not at a Super 8.

Pricing is a prime example of why knowing and defining your brand is so important. What's the difference between a $1,000-a-night hotel and a $75-a-night hotel? A lot. As a business owner, you need to know those differences, know which type you want to be, and then own your prices that align with your brand.

Now that you are an ace at understanding profit margins and pricing, I invite you to take a look at your current products or services and calculate the profit margins of each item or service you sell. After you have done this, notice which items or services are big money-makers for you (and which are not). Then ask yourself if you can sell more of the money-makers. If so, how will you do that? Next, ask yourself if the items or services with low profitability can be adjusted to bring in better margins. Can you increase the prices on them? Also ask yourself if they are worth continuing or if you should consider phasing them out.

After considering those questions, start working on sales projections. I have provided sample sales projections for you at kdawsonco.com/resources. Use them to either improve your current profitability, create your future profitability, or create a revenue plan for your new business. (I recommend you wait until after you have read Chapter 6 and Chapter 7 before completing your sales projections.)

Note: This may seem self explanatory, but I have known people to confuse projections with actual sales. Sales projections are not *actual sales, but rather estimates of what you* might *see in the future, based on past and current sales. They can also be based on what you plan to accomplish in the upcoming months and years, after considering new marketing plans, or directional changes in your business.*

When I create sales projections for clients, I often include three separate sets of projections: conservative, moderate, and aggressive. Conservative projections show the least amount of sales, and aggressive projections show ideal sales. It's good to look at this range to get an idea of what to expect, knowing that the actual projections may be closest to the middle, or moderate, estimates.

CHAPTER 6

CREATE YOUR BRAND

TRUE OR FALSE: YOUR BRAND IS YOUR LOGO, your elevator pitch, your website, or your business card.

You know the answer: FALSE.

These items should *communicate* your brand, but they are not your brand itself.

Your brand is *you!*

The term *brand* gets used a lot in the entrepreneurial sphere, so what exactly is it, and how is it defined? If you search online for the definition you will most likely find several different ones, but I think brand can be summed up by saying it is what identifies you to others. Your brand is unique to you, and when others see it, they know that it is your brand. When others can identify you without being *told* it is you, that is when you have built a solid brand.

A few examples would be when you see a certain design, whether a piece of furniture, a handbag, or a pair of shoes, and you know who the designer is without seeing their logo or name. Most people familiar with IKEA furniture can identify their products without being told it is IKEA. The same goes for Crate and Barrel, West Elm, and Pottery Barn. You can say the same about a Coach handbag or a pair of Jessica Simpson shoes. Fans of these brands can identify them easily, because they can recognize their style, distinguishing characteristics, and consistency of design.

A brand can then be described as everything that you "put out there" in the market that displays or communicates your style, distinguishes you from others, and also demonstrates consistency. What you put out there includes your logo, company colors, website, and business cards, but it includes much more.

Your brand also identifies your values. Your values can be communicated through the quality of what you put out there. If you value professionalism, your brand will be professional. You might wear a suit and conduct business in a serious, professional manner. Your branding materials might include traditional colors and a simple design. If you value fun and adventure, your brand might use bold and bright colors, and include funky designs, and you might dress more fashionably and less traditional.

The important takeaway is to be able to define your brand—your values, your style, and distinguishing characteristics—and create a consistent image of these throughout everything you create, sell, and produce, including your branding materials such as your logo, website, product packaging, colors, and marketing collateral.

Now that you hopefully have an understanding of what a *brand* is, you need to learn how to discover and define yours. Your brand begins to form an identity once you allow it to be authentically you. What makes you unique will also be what sets you apart from your competition. You can articulate who you are, what you offer, and why you matter to those who need you through your brand. This will draw people to you and create a business that thrives.

START WITH WHO YOU ARE

Asking you to identify what makes you *you* is a daunting question that can be difficult to answer. Many of us struggle to know who we are. This is in part due to being bombarded with images our entire lives, though film, media, work, school, friends, and family, telling us who we *should* be, which can distract us from seeing who we really are.

In order to see clearly through the weeds, you need to remove any judgments or criticisms you have about yourself. Understand that everything about you is what makes you who you are. Your choices, good and bad, your experiences, your values, your passions—all contribute to who you are today. And it's all good.

To use this information to help you build your brand, clear your mind of the *should bes* and the judgments, and ask yourself to define **your passions** (what inspires and moves you), **your values** (what and who you care about, consistently and unconditionally), **your purpose** (who you want to help and how you want to contribute to the world), and **your skills** (what you do exceptionally well).

I am passionate about____.

I value ____.

My purpose is ____.

My best skills are_______________________________________.

Example:

I am passionate about entrepreneurship, freedom, fulfillment, achievement, wealth, creativity, growth, and family.

I value my children; being a caring, supportive, and loving mother; integrity, kindness, empathy, education, and independence.

My purpose is to help women live happy, fulfilling lives where they have the freedom to excel in their careers, as well as in their personal lives, and to enjoy the rewards that financial success can bring them: independence, freedom, and power.

My best skills are being a strategic thinker, organized, good at planning, mathematical and analytical, a problem-solver, an effective teacher, empathetic, and intelligent; having good listening skills, management and operational skills, and experience working within various industries.

Now that you've read mine, you can see how all four of these tie into what I do as a business strategist who primarily works with women, teaching them how to grow their businesses, specifically as it relates to revenue generation and financial success, which can give them the freedom to live the lives they choose, and have both a successful career and time for their children and family. My work and my brand are in sync with who I am as a person.

When you start to build your own brand, you want to be able to achieve this type of synergy between you and your brand.

Do this exercise for yourself and compare it to your current brand. Are you where you should be, or do you need to better develop and define your brand?

DEVELOP YOUR BRAND

Now that you've defined who you are and what you value, it's time to translate that into developing your brand. Take your passions, values, purpose, and skills, and let them *become* your brand. They say that most of us start businesses in an effort to actually help ourselves with what *we* need. Keep this in mind as you develop your brand. It will help you later with your marketing strategies.

Getting more specific with the activity we did in Chapter 1 and using your responses above to guide you, answer the following:

Who do you want to help? ______________________________________

Why do you want to help them?______________________________________

How will you help them? ______________________________________

Example:

Who: I want to help ambitious female entrepreneurs looking to make their businesses more profitable and sustainable.

Why: Because as an ambitious entrepreneurial woman myself, who is also a divorced mother, I know how important it is to be able to earn your own money, create your own wealth, and be able to provide yourself and your family with both resources and time. Entrepreneurship allows me to make a significant amount of money, while also giving me the freedom to schedule my own time.

How: By using my knowledge, skills, and experience, I can teach women the business skills needed to understand, manage, and grow their businesses better and smarter. I can analyze their businesses from a technical and financial perspective to provide sound advice and guidance in order to help them make better decisions.

You can see by my answers, clarifying who I am as a person and what I value translates into my brand, which translates into my business purpose and whom I wish to help.

When you do this exercise, think about your answers through fresh eyes. Don't just write down what you currently think. Part of the purpose of this exercise is to get you thinking from a new perspective and to challenge what you may have previously thought about your business brand. You may come to the same conclusions about your purpose and who you wish to serve, but perhaps you won't. Give yourself the opportunity to gain new clarity around your brand and market.

You have your branding right when the message you send to your audience accurately represents who you are and your target market clearly understands how you can help them. With this, a connection is made.

SEND THE RIGHT MESSAGE

Sending the right message is very important—and, quite frankly, a common area where I see business owners mess up. So how do you make sure you are sending the right message?

You should be sending a consistent message throughout the many aspects of your business. These aspects include not just your logo, website, and product packaging, but can also be identified by the "peers you keep": your business partners, employees, contractors, and customers. Your brand can also be found in they way you speak, write, carry yourself, and treat others.

So where do I see people mess up? In the most blunt terms, they cheap out on their branding, which results in having inconsistent messaging that doesn't represent their values.

If you want to create a company that is viewed as high quality, for example, it needs to show in your branding (and pricing!). You can't have a website that looks like an amateur designed it (or that you self-created in a template people have seen 1,000 times over). You can't have a high-priced product in cheap packaging, and you can't conduct business in a place that looks like a rusty, un-insulated car garage if customers visit you.

This goes beyond quality. It also relates to the characteristics customers expect from you. If you are an accountant, you should be highly detail-oriented, so if your marketing content is full of errors, you will send the message that you will also miss details in clients' finances. If you market yourself as a graphic designer but you can't use Photoshop like a boss, you can't possibly be a good designer.

Everything you create and do needs to match your brand, even if it means spending more money than you'd like and investing more time than you think you have. There *are* areas of your business where you can save money, but branding shouldn't be one of them.

Branding is an area in which you need to be willing to spend money. Hire the best people you can find to help you craft your message so that it is the best it can be.

To be clear, I'm not saying that if you sell quality items or services you need to spend $30K on a website. I am saying that every aspect of your business that represents your brand should be consistent with your brand and with your values. If you pride yourself on providing quality, everything you put out there should also be quality.

THE COMPANY YOU KEEP

Let's return for a moment to "the company you keep." Many people, as they build their professional network, tend to get connected to new people by people they already know. If the people in your immediate circle do not match your brand, then you will be continuing to build a bigger network of people who also don't match your brand. Before you know it, you will be surrounded by people who don't match your brand, and your business will surely suffer.

Take the time to start building your network around the people most in sync with you and your brand, and focus on building around, and from, them. Don't be afraid to say *no* to networking groups and events that don't mesh with your brand. Spending time with people who won't or can't help you build your business is not helpful. Think about this every time you get an invite to an event or even when connecting on social media. Truly, your success depends on the company you keep.

DO YOUR PRODUCTS OR SERVICES MATCH YOUR BRAND?

Before moving on to defining your market, look at your offerings. Make sure they represent and match your brand. Create a table similar to the following that lists your current products or services, with their respective price, and ask yourself if everything is in alignment. Do your current offerings match up?

Product/Service	Price	Who does it currently appeal to?	Does it match your brand, value, ideal customer, and overall vision?

Example:

Public Speaking & Communications Coach for Business Professionals and Corporate Executives

Product/Service	Price	Who does it currently appeal to?	Does it match your brand, value, ideal customer, and overall vision?
Private coaching lessons	$5,000 for 3 months	Business executives and professionals	YES
Workshops at co-share workspace	Free	Freelancers and startup entrepreneurs	NO
Breakout sessions at corporate conventions	$10,000 per event	Corporate executives and employees	YES
Breakout sessions at wellness conferences	$500 per event	Yoga instructors, nutritionists, and personal trainers	NO

This is your opportunity to review your current offerings with a fine-tooth comb and ensure that what you offer makes sense. If it does, great! If it doesn't, it may be time to make some changes.

For example, I once posted on a Facebook group that I belonged to that I was looking for someone to hire who worked in sales and marketing. I received inquiries from several independent contractors who owned their own businesses as social media or marketing professionals, or even as personal assistants. One inquiry in particular stood out to me. Her email inquiring about my need for an assistant/marketing professional was full of typos, uncapitalized "i's," and several emoticons. (I was tempted to write back and offer her advice on this, but decided not to for obvious reasons.)

The point is simple: If you sell services as a writer, content creator, or professional assistant, everything you put out there needs to be top notch. No spelling errors, no typos, and no grammatical mistakes. If you sell shoes for $300, they should come in a good-quality box, with a stylish logo, and last for several years to come. They should be sold in stores where I would expect to find them, alongside $600 dresses and $1,000 suits. A $20 pair of shoes, on the other hand, may not even come in a box at all and instead may be found hanging on a rack, with the pair held together by an elastic string and a paper price tag. I don't expect these shoes to last past the end of summer.

When you look at your brand and the company image you are trying to build, make sure everything you put out there matches. If you want to have a high-quality brand, you need to charge high-quality fees while not cheaping out on what you put out there and invest in for your business. The reverse is also true: Don't invest everything you have into your business trying to build a quality brand, then charge peanuts for your products or services. If you're selling lipstick for $5, I'm going to think it isn't top quality. If you sell it for $25, I'm going to think it's good stuff. Your prices need to be in line with your brand.

In summary, as you create and develop your brand, remember your brand should communicate a unified and consistent message to your audience telling them who you are, what you stand for, and how you are unique. It should also tell them who *they* are and how you can help them. Your marketing, prices, network, and quality of work all communicate this message. Make sure they accurately represent your brand.

CHAPTER 7

DEFINE YOUR MARKET

NOW THAT YOU'VE IDENTIFIED YOU AND YOUR BRAND, it's time to identify your customer. So, who is your target audience? The answer should never be "anyone who will buy from me."

One of the biggest mistakes small business owners make, especially in the first few years of their business, is feeling so desperate for business that they take any client that comes along. Their social media marketing is all over the place; they're blasting out videos, posts, and images everywhere they can; and they have no strategy around attracting a specific audience. The idea is that if they blast info everywhere, eventually someone will bite.

I get it: You really need to make some money and you don't want to turn down any opportunity for potential business, and you don't know how else to get attention. However, the problem isn't about getting noticed.

While it may seem scary at first, the best way to build your business is to define your specific market, intentionally seek them out, and say *no* to those who don't align. The more you focus, the more you stand out.

If you're not yet convinced, let me put it to you another way. Small business owners are, well . . . small. They lack resources such as money and time, and often need staff or workers, whom they can't afford, to help. It's not uncommon to be a one-woman show where you alone are responsible for creating your product or service, as well as doing most (if not all) of the sales, marketing, admin work, communications, networking, and so on. Every task falls on you (though we'll talk more about delegating later in the book). Even if you do have help, you are still probably strapped most of the time regarding resources, feeling like you never have enough money, time, or help from others.

In this scenario, if you build your business to appeal to the masses, you will not only stretch your resources too thin, you will be ineffective at nearly everything you do. By defining a specific market, or creating a niche, you will not only be able to conserve your resources, but will have a better chance of standing out in a competitive crowd.

Let's look at an example. Say it's a hot summer day and your younger self is ready to set up a lemonade stand. You live in a large neighborhood where everyone else is setting up their lemonade stands. You realize that your neighborhood is filled with many different kinds of people. Some are older, and some are younger. Some jog or walk every day for exercise, while others sit on the porch having a beer and smoking a cigarette.

You decide that you are going to sell your lemonade to the runners who are health conscious and are willing to pay higher prices for natural food and beverages. So rather than selling the same artificially flavored, cheap powdered mix that everyone else is selling, you make freshly squeezed lemonade with organic sugar served with fresh mint leaves. I guarantee you, no one else on the block is doing this.

By offering a different version of an ordinary product, you will get noticed by the runners who see your sign that says "Fresh-Squeezed Lemonade with Organic Sugar and a Hint of Mint." You will have less competition because you are the only one on the block selling this version of a common item, and you'll make more money because your audience is willing to pay a premium for natural, organic lemonade.

This is exactly how it works when you choose a specific audience, recognizing their wants and needs as well as their traits and characteristics, and create a product or service specifically for them.

Step back a moment and look at how you responded to the questions in the Develop Your Brand section in Chapter 6, where we discussed identifying who you want to help, why you want to help them, and how will you help them. With these responses in mind, let's tweak them a bit and complete the following:

I WANT TO HELP ______________________________

(your target audience)

BY OFFERING______________________________

(your service or product)

BECAUSE THIS WILL GIVE THEM ______________________

(what they gain from your offering/the benefit they receive).

Thinking about who you want to help, how you will help them, and what they need from you should help you break down the specific details of your market. Here are characteristics to consider when defining your market.

- ❑ Consumer or Business

  One of the simplest questions to ask yourself should be whether you want to sell to consumers (B2C) or to other businesses (B2B). If you're thinking you'd like to do both, let me just say . . .

  Don't.

  Why? Because marketing to consumers is completely different from marketing to businesses. Always keep in mind your marketing efforts. Marketing is one of the most difficult aspects of running a business, and you make it twice as hard, and twice as costly, when you spend time and money marketing to two different audiences.

There are pros and cons to selling to each market. With B2B you are dealing with other businesses who understand that spending and investing are part of day-to-day business. Therefore they might be more apt to purchase from you, and they have larger budgets available to them. Marketing can also be easier with B2B due to the vast opportunities of in-person networking, trade shows, conferences, and other arenas for business professionals to congregate.

In contrast, B2C can be difficult because individuals are more protective over their personal funds compared to businesses, and they do not usually have the large budget that a business would have. Marketing to them can also be more difficult because you can't market to them the same way you can B2B. For example, attending a networking event or conference where you exchange business cards is completely acceptable, but going to a friend's home or party and handing out your business cards to the guests can be off-putting and intrusive.

On the flip side, there are benefits of B2C that B2B doesn't have. With B2C, since you are selling personal goods to consumers, branding, marketing, and selling can feel more personal and genuine, and less corporate. You are appealing to what people love or need, not what a corporation needs. Marketing can also be easier, because we are *all* consumers and we know what works and what doesn't, intuitively.

Another benefit of B2C is it might be easier to break into your industry, with more access to resources, and with lower startup costs. This is not always the case, but it can be, depending on your business. For example, if you wanted to start your own interior design business (B2C), you could create a website for a few hundred dollars, start emailing your friends and posting on social media about your new services, and reach out to specific people you know asking if they'd be interested in hiring you. Eventually, you get your first client, start making some money, and get referred to another client, and your business builds organically with little up-front cost or resources needed.

In contrast, a B2B business might involve creating a software program to sell to companies in the financial industry. This would involve raising capital to pay for developers, rent for office space, and research. You would also need to be making connections with financial companies, pitching your software to people you don't know, and hoping they offer to buy your product before it is even developed. Of course there are B2C businesses that can be just as difficult as the software company, such as launching a children's toy company—and there can be B2B businesses that are much easier to launch, such as graphic design services, that would be similar to the interior designer. The point is, both B2B and B2C can be good options, but for small businesses it is better to choose one that works best for your brand and stick with it.

- [ ] Age

More likely than not, your business and brand will appeal to a particular age group.

Try to think about what age group your target market is, because the strategies you use for marketing to someone in their 40s will be different from those marketing to someone in their 20s. Based on my experience, I have made the following observations:

Regarding social media, Millennials seem more likely to use platforms such as Snapchat or Instagram, whereas Gen Xers tend to prefer Facebook or Twitter. Baby Boomers seem more likely to use Facebook if they are on social media but may not necessarily use social media at all.

Millennials might be more likely to consume a lot of information, superficially (scrolling through feeds all day), whereas Gen Xers might be more inclined to be purpose-driven with their use of social media and seek out only what interests them. Millennials also seem more likely than not to communicate via texting or messaging, whereas Gen Xers might prefer in-person communication, email, or phone. Baby Boomers might also prefer phone and in-person communication.

Other differences can be found in their spending habits and the values they have around money. My generation (the 'Xers) was raised to focus on building savings, investing in a home, and acquiring education and assets. Millennials, in contrast, seem to prefer spending money on experiences, rather than acquiring assets.

Again, these are my general observations, but the takeaway is that you need to consider the age group whom you are selling to, and how and where they consume information (online or in-person), which online platform(s) they prefer, and what their values around spending money are.

- [ ] Education

This one can get tricky, but sometimes a particular product or service will appeal to primarily those with a certain education level. This not only refers to whether you have a doctorate degree, but it also refers to how much education one would have in a particular subject area.

For example, suppose you sell an extensive line of nutritional supplements, including specific herbs, extracts, and botanicals. The average person isn't going to know what half of your products are, or what they are used for, and therefore these products have no value to them. Your market will be those consumers who have an interest, as well as ongoing education in the areas of natural medicine and nutritional products.

- [ ] Industry

Do your products or services appeal to a particular industry, or a few specific industries? This one can be like an onion, in that you have to peel back a few layers. On the surface, you might assume your brand isn't industry specific, but it may be *better* if it were.

Like our lemonade example, choosing to focus on a particular niche group can help you stand out and be seen as a specialist or an expert in your field.

Regardless of what you sell, take a moment to consider choosing one to three industries in which you could specialize.

- ☐ Life Stage

Similar to age, this category looks at your customers' life stage. Are they single, married, married with children, divorced?

Do they own their first home, own their last home, rent? Are they working full-time, retired, in school? The list goes on. Like the other categories, the further you can narrow this down, the better. And again, for the same reason, it makes your marketing efforts much easier and cheaper.

As a mother of school-aged children, I pack my kids' lunches every day. I usually include a warm thermos along with cold items like milk and fruit. My issue is that I want to keep the thermos warm and the cold stuff cold, but I have to put them in the same lunch box. Right now I use a large cloth napkin to separate them. One of my grand business ideas would be to create a lunch box where half of it can be warm and the other half cold.

(If you decide it's the business for you, please let me know where I can buy one!)

The point is, if this were your product, your life stage market would be mothers of school-aged children. This is a pretty specific group. What life stage do your products most appeal to?

- ☐ Beliefs

While this does not apply to all businesses, your offerings might resonate with people who share certain beliefs (political, religious, moral, etc.).

Take a moment to consider if your products are most valued by people sharing a particular set of beliefs. For example, I belonged to a mastermind group where someone in the group was launching a business selling fashionable but modest clothing for women. She believed there were not many options for women who prefer to dress more modestly or conservatively. She decided to launch an online clothing store offering women a place to purchase clothing that was stylish, but would also accommodate their preference for modest attire.

- [ ] Geography

Does your business/brand/product appeal to people in a certain area? Or maybe a type of area such as rural, urban, or suburban?

This one is also an onion—and takes more thought than you might think. For example, I spend a lot of time in two different cities, each with different cultures, values, lifestyles, and economics. Many of the businesses that I see in one city could never survive in the other, due to these differences, and vice versa.

I also suggest that small businesses choose a particular geographic area to focus on the beginning. As you grow, expand to new areas. For example, if you were in my area you might start in Boston, then expand to the surrounding areas within the state, then branch out to all of New England, followed by the Northeast.

- [ ] Skills

This is a simple one. It refers to any particular skills your audience might have or need. For example, if you're selling software for graphic designers, what skills will they have in order to have a need for your product?

- [ ] Values

When I use the term *values,* I'm not referring to the beliefs listed above. I'm referring to things like quality or quantity, luxury or economical, casual or sophisticated, trendy or sustainable, convenience or organic.

For example, some people seek out locally grown and made foods, and are willing to pay a premium for them because they value supporting local farmers, or getting their food as close to natural as possible. This could mean purchasing milk and meat from local farmers, or buying skincare products made with local honey. However, others are more driven by price when it comes to food and would prefer to see milk on sale for $1.99 a gallon or be able to buy in bulk to get wholesale prices.

Know what your market values. This will help you decide what kinds of products or services to offer, how to price them, how to package them, and how to appeal to your audience.

- [ ] Financial Status

This should be obvious, but the financial status of your target market will depend on what you sell. If you are selling a high-priced item, you know your market will need to be above a certain income bracket.

- [ ] Interests

This question isn't really related to your product, but is more about identifying the interests of your target audience.

For example, suppose you sell skincare products for women. From this you could assume that your audience may also be interested in fashion, health, or anti-aging products. Therefore, if you were going to choose a venue to sell your products, you might choose to do a pop-up shop at a fashion show or at a health and wellness fair.

- [ ] Needs

Finally, what do they need? If you are a life coach, your audience needs clarity, peace of mind, fulfillment, satisfaction in life, and happiness. You need to think about what types of people are looking for these in their lives and how you can incorporate solutions to them in your marketing efforts.

It's Your Turn

Complete the following to create the detailed description of your target audience:

1. Consumer or Business ______________________________

2. Age ______________________________

3. Education ______________________________

4. Industry ______________________________

5. Life Stage ______________________________

6. Beliefs ______________________________

7. Geography ______________________________

8. Skills ______________________________

9. Values ______________________________

10. Financial Status ______________________________

11. Interests ______________________________

12. Needs ______________________________

CREATE YOUR CUSTOMER PROFILE

Now that you've given a detailed description of your target audience, you can take it a step further and create your customer profile. This is a fictitious character you create to give life to your target audience. Here's an example.

Product: Online Time Management and Project Planning Software

Target Audience: Entrepreneurs looking to gain control over their day, be more productive, feel less stressed, and improve their ability to manage projects and achieve their business goals. They are between the ages of late 20s and early 50s, they are college-educated, and they work in client-based industries. They like to be organized, are goal-oriented, and value productivity, progress, and achievement, as well as doing quality work for their clients. They are in the mid- to upper-middle income range with a salary from their business exceeding $80,000 per year, and an average closer to $150,000. They care about their clients and want to provide as much value as possible for what they are paid. They care about time management and having enough time to work, as well as spend time with their families. They want a product that is detail-oriented, practical, useful, easy-to-use, efficient, and flexible. They need to be supported in working on their projects, keeping on schedule for achieving their goals, and managing their time.

Customer Profile: Susie is in her early 40s, is married with three school-aged children, and started her own interior design business about five years ago. She primarily works with corporate clients designing large spaces such as restaurants, eateries, and cafés. She works from home but travels occasionally to meet with clients and visit her projects. In order for her to be successful she needs help managing all of her client files, projects, vendors, and contracts. She also needs a system for organizing her samples (textile swatches, lighting fixtures, and some artwork). She doesn't use social media much, as most of her business is referral-based due to her specialty. Her technology needs are around automating her processes of creating proposals, quotes, and contracts, and managing each of her projects. She lives in the suburbs of Manhattan, about a 30- to 40-minute drive from the city in Westchester County. Her children attend private school and her husband is an attorney for an international paper company.

When you read through this profile, you should begin to create an image in your mind of the ideal customer for this business. Not only is there a specific description of the group, but even an example of a typical consumer of the product.

Creating a detailed description, and even a sample customer profile, can be extremely helpful when marketing your services or products. Doing so allows you to think about someone in particular, which in turn leads to a much easier answer to the question of "Where can I find them?"

In this example, where do you think we could find Susie? Keep in mind the product is a software product (a SAAS product to be exact) and not a brick-and-mortar or service product, which makes this a little trickier. You're not going to advertise at her kids' school, or at her local fitness gym, or on a billboard during her commute to the city. Where is Susie spending her time that would make sense for an online product?

Here are a few possibilities:

- ❑ **Trade shows:** Since Susie is in the design industry, which relies on continuously being introduced to new ideas, new products, new interior apparel, and new styles, someone like Susie is going to attend at least one trade show per year, where she will shop multiple vendors in her industry. Having a booth at these types of industry events could be a perfect place for this business. As hundreds, if not thousands, of consultants just like Susie are shopping around the expo floor, your software demo is on display for all to see.

- ❑ **Targeted online advertising:** This one could get pricey, but with the right budget, and the right target, you could advertise alongside other software products that are in synergy with yours, using the appropriate keywords that someone like Susie would use.

- ❑ **Partner with industry conferences:** This could be offering to host a workshop, sponsor an event, or speak at a conference on topics related to your software, such as time management or project management. This might entail getting an agent to represent you, so you look more professional, or creating a kickass media kit that really sells you to these conferences. Again, Susie is going to attend these at least once a year to continue her education in the field of business, consulting, and design. She may also attend in an effort to find herself clients, which brings me to . . .

- ❑ **Attending industry specific events to network:** You could consider attending industry-specific events simply to network and meet potential customers.

Notice that all four of these involve presenting or networking with a national audience, which may be necessary for an online software, SAAS-based company. Also notice that they involve being very specific toward your market.

Of course, every service or product is different, and depending on what you sell will determine where you can find your market. Questions you should ask yourself about your target market include:

- ❑ Where do they shop?
- ❑ Where do they live?
- ❑ Where do they work?
- ❑ Where do they spend most of their time?
- ❑ How much do they use social media? (More on this later.)
- ❑ Which social media platforms do they use most?
- ❑ What do they read?
- ❑ What do they listen to?

At this point you may be wondering why I am getting *so* detailed about all of this. Here's why:

Many business owners, especially newer, less-established ones, don't take the time to think about where their ideal clients are spending their time, so they waste a lot of time being in the wrong places.

Tell me if this sounds familiar. You own a business and you're told you need to get out there and "network." Perhaps you're a consultant, a coach, a financial advisor, a real estate agent; the list goes on. So you sign up for every event you hear about from the chamber of commerce to a local professional women's networking group, only to discover you almost never get business out of any of them. Why?

One of the reasons is because you're not really narrowing down your market, creating your ideal customer profile, and asking yourself where they are (and then being there).

For example, suppose you own a concierge service and you're looking for new clients. You attend a local networking group of women artisans who sell arts and crafts. Most likely this group will not be needing your services. They might not be in the income bracket necessary to spend their disposable income on a personal assistant. They also may not be in need of one, as they have flexible schedules. However, a networking group full of corporate executives who are juggling full-time management positions, family, and community responsibilities might be a smarter place for you to network.

Too many small business owners don't take the time to accurately describe their market and ideal customer, and the results are a lot of wasted time and unneeded stress, spinning wheels, and wondering why things aren't happening for them. Don't be that person.

It's Your Turn

Now that you've had a chance to look at an in-depth example, it's your turn to take your detailed target market, create your client profile, and then ask yourself where you would find them. Brainstorm a few ideas using the questions stated above to help guide you.

MY CUSTOMER PROFILE EXERCISE

My Product: (Describe what you sell.)

My Target Audience: (Detail characteristics of your target market, including demographics such as age, where they live, occupation, education level, and economic status, as well as their interests, values, and needs.)

My Customer Profile: (Give your ideal client or customer a name and persona. Where does she live, how old is she, what is her occupation, what does she value, what is her lifestyle like, how many hours per week does she work, where does she work, how does she spend her time, where does she get her information from, and what does she need to make her life and/or business better?)

CHAPTER 8

CONNECT WITH YOUR MARKET

LET'S REGROUP. You have defined your brand, your market, and your ideal customer. You also came up with a few ideas about where you can find them. The next step is to figure out how you will connect with them and turn them into quality leads.

In my opinion, lead generation is the most difficult aspect of running your business, at least in the first few years, as you're trying to create something that didn't previously exist. For some, lead generation is an ongoing process, no matter how long you've been in business.

Without leads, there are no sales, and without sales, there is no business.

Your job as a small business owner is to create a system that is efficient and effective at generating quality leads, converting them into sales, and satisfying them so they come back for more—and are excited enough that they refer you to new leads.

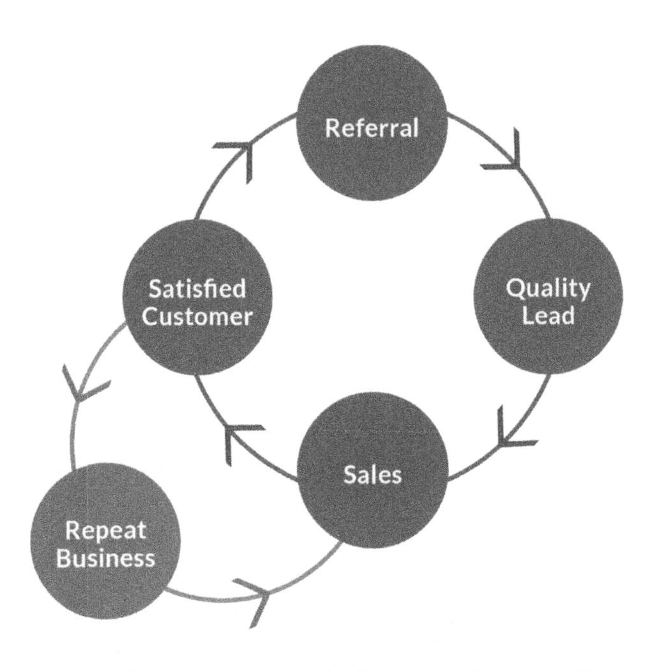

In order to effectively generate quality leads, you need to empathize with your customer as much as possible, putting yourself in their shoes to determine what they need and want. Here are three steps you can take to accomplish this, using my business as an example:

1. Make a list of places your ideal customer might be, where you can also be. This includes online and in-person. An example might be trade shows or conferences, as stated in Chapter 7. You can start with a generic list ("conferences"), and then get more specific (naming specific conferences to attend). This step will involve some research on your part, but will get you results.

   I work primarily with entrepreneurial women who are always seeking networking opportunities and learning opportunities around how to grow their business. They are too busy working to attend monthly meetings, but they will attend the occasional annual conference. Specifically, they look for conferences geared toward entrepreneurial women and focused on topics around growing their business and building their network.

   I'm putting myself in their shoes, knowing what they need and where they look for solutions (and again, where they spend their time).

2. Ask yourself what problems they have for which you can provide solutions. Think of your market, what they need, and how you can help them.

   *Getting more specific about my clients' needs, I ask myself **how** they want to grow their business and **what** specifically they need to do that. Usually they need help scaling their business, so they can grow financially without having to work 1,000 hours a week; they want to hire help and focus on running their business, which will reduce their stress levels and how many tasks are on their to-do list; they want to make more money to fund growth; and if they are building a product-based business they may want to learn how to get their products on national retail shelves or how to build a large audience for their online store. I can help them by teaching them the knowledge, skills, and strategies needed to accomplish these goals. My methods of teaching include workshops and classes, webinars, and consulting.*

3. Brainstorm methods you can use to capture their interest and get their attention.

   Using the conference example, I have a few choices on how to capture their interest.

   a. *I can apply to be a speaker or lead a workshop at a conference.*

   b. *I can offer to sponsor a conference by providing free copies of my book in their swag bags and/or by financially supporting the conference as a sponsor.*

   c. *I can choose to attend a conference as an attendee and focus my efforts on networking and meeting people.*

   To choose which of these three is best, weigh the pros and cons of each and determine which will give you the best return on investment (ROI). Compare the cost of each to you to the expected number of clients/sales dollars you would generate from each and compute which one would give you the best results.

Following is an example using fictitious numbers. Suppose there are 250 attendees at this conference. Here are two possible scenarios:

1. The cost of swag bag books = $2,500 (250 × $10 per book). This could result in one client at $10,000.

2. The cost to attend = $250. This could result in three clients from networking, or $30,000.

In this case, you'd be better off going to network, where people have the opportunity to meet you and connect with you, as opposed to paying a lot of money as a swag bag sponsor and most likely getting little return from that.

Of course, there would be other things to consider if this were a real scenario. If you were selling an online course, and there was a promo code in the books for it, you could possibly get 50 attendees signing up for your online course that costs $1,000 each, which would bring in $50,000—a better ROI. The likelihood of that is slim to none, but you get the point.

From this exercise, you can see how I've gone from analyzing my ideal customer, determining what they need and why/how I can help, asking where they can be found, and generating ideas on how I can get their attention and connect with them.

Use these steps to guide you for both your overall strategic marketing plan, as well as the specific components to your marketing plan (such as the example regarding conferences). Once you begin to write all of this out, you will have the foundation of your marketing plan.

YOUR MARKETING PLAN

The purpose of having a marketing plan is to help you acquire customers in a strategic way so that your time and money are both well spent. Without a plan, you are more likely to spend money you shouldn't trying to promote your business in the wrong places, or waste time trying to get the attention of those who are not in your market. With a plan, you can get specific about your customer acquisition goals and create action items to help you achieve those goals. If you've been "winging it" with your marketing, having a plan that tells you what to do and when to do it, will be much less work.

Building your marketing plan will be much easier if you have defined your market, created your ideal customer profile, and identified where you can find them. Once you have these pieces, you can begin to set marketing goals and action plans. The first step is to set marketing goals that are realistic and progressive. I'll discuss goal setting more in Chapter 11, but for now, start by setting a goal that creating an action plan to go with it that you can achieve within a certain time frame.

For example, suppose you have launched a business services firm. You provide your clients with accounting and bookkeeping needs, as well as payroll processing and virtual office management. Your target audience are small businesses with fewer than 30 employees, and you primarily work with retail owners such as cafés, small restaurants, and boutique shops. These businesses are typically found in small, downtown areas within a 25-mile radius of your home. Your customer profile is described as middle-aged, extremely busy from running their business six to seven days a week, not very profitable, and needing help with the finances and business planning side of things because they are too busy in the day-to-day operations.

You started your business one year ago, and currently have four clients who each pay you $800 each per month for your services. Your revenue goal is twice this amount, so you need to have eight clients each month. Therefore, you need to create your marketing plan with the goal of acquiring four new monthly clients within the next six months.

After determining this goal, now it's time to break down this goal into a plan. When creating your marketing plan, look at the various marketing vehicles, and determine which ones you will use and how you will use them. This includes asking yourself if you will focus more on inbound marketing or outbound marketing.

Outbound marketing refers to traditional forms of marketing such as cold calling, direct mail, and door-to-door salespeople. Outbound marketing also includes paid advertisements such as print ads, but also online ads like banner ads and Google ads. While there is still a place for outbound marketing in several industries (real estate is one of them), outbound marketing has been replaced with *inbound marketing* in recent years.

Inbound marketing refers to strategies that involve bringing people to you, rather than you going directly after them. The idea is that rather than directly selling to them (outbound), you offer them useful content, share stories, and create experiences to get them interested in you, and then they seek *you* out to learn more about what you have to offer. Examples include writing blog articles, posting videos, offering free e-books, and sharing tips and advice on social media.

One of the main reasons (if not *the* main reason) for the move from outbound to inbound marketing is that outbound is much more costly. Print advertising can cost thousands, even tens of thousands, of dollars, whereas writing a blog article and posting it online is free (with the exception of the relatively nominal expense of hosting your own blog). Once people realized they could essentially advertise online and be seen by the masses without it costing a dime, the advertising and marketing industry changed dramatically, and business hasn't been the same since.

Back to your marketing plan. You'll need to consider these various marketing vehicles and which ones you will use to achieve your goals. In our example of the business services firm, you know your market, but you need to determine how you will attract their attention and get them to sign on as a new client. To do this, start generating ideas around these marketing vehicles. Ask yourself what makes the most sense to connect with your audience.

Your thought process might look something like this: Your target audience is absorbed in the day-to-day operations of running a retail business, which means they most likely do not attend networking or social events. They may or may not spend a lot of time on social media, and their customers mostly come from foot traffic and web searches (such as when someone searched "dry cleaning near me"), so they may not have as much incentive to do their own online marketing.

In this case, spending the majority of *your* time online marketing may or may not be beneficial. You might fair better by building relationships with other businesses that they already know and that use their services—and be referred to them instead. For example, you could build up your network of attorneys and CPAs or tax accountants, share with them the services you provide for retail businesses, and ask if they have any clients that could use your services.

If the businesses you wish to work with spend time online, and also market their own businesses online, you can build into your marketing plan strategies around how to get their attention in the platforms you think they would use, by providing content they would be interested in.

You could also consider doing a small, inexpensive, direct mail campaign to a very targeted audience. Response rates to direct mail are very low (1–3%), but if you only need four clients, and you send a 50-cent postcard to 200 local businesses, it would cost $100 in postage and a few hundred dollars in design and printing, but might give you a new, long-term client who will provide you with $800 per month for the next several years. Seems like an idea worth trying, at least once.

After going through these various ideas, your marketing plan would begin to develop. You begin by stating your goal and creating a broad action plan, followed by breaking down the details of each action item into specific to-do tasks with deadlines. It might look something like this:

GOAL:

Retain 4 new clients within next 6 months (pick a date)

ACTION PLAN:

1. Attend 1 or 2 networking events each month that attract those in professional services, such as legal, accounting, tax, insurance, finance, and

others. Focus on making meaningful connections with follow up 1–3 days after each event. Purpose is to build a referral network. Directly ask each person I meet if they know of anyone who could benefit from my services, and if they do, ask for an email introduction.

2. Research all local retail businesses within a 25-mile radius that would be a good fit. Make a list of them, and engage with them on Facebook and Instagram. If they use social media, they most likely are using visual platforms like Instagram to show their products. Do more than like their page or profile; engage with them and even offer a free template to help them with their business budget or give them an info sheet on tips for retaining employees and having less turnover. Ask for nothing in return.

3. Research fellow business service professionals and find ways to engage with them online. Perhaps join a few online communities where building a referral network is encouraged. Build relationships in these communities so that when they have a client or hear of someone looking for help with their business, they think of you.

4. Create a direct mailing for 200 local, small business retailers in your community offering a free consultation to discuss their business needs. Hire a talented graphic designer to make the card eye-catching, modern, and appealing enough to actually be read.

TO-DO ITEMS/TIME LINE

- ❑ Sign up for 6 networking events over first 3 months, and 6 events for remaining 3 months.

- ❑ Create follow-up email for each person I meet and send within 1–3 days of networking event.

- ❑ Choose a small group, perhaps 3–6 people, that I connected with and work on building a relationship with them by inviting them to other events, engaging with them online, or asking for more information about their services and seeing if there is a way to help them (maybe tell others in your network about them).

- [ ] Follow 10 new businesses a day, 5 days per week.
- [ ] Engage with 5 new businesses per day, 5 days per week.
- [ ] Join 3 online communities and engage at least once per week in each group.
- [ ] Generate 3 topic ideas for downloadable content materials (tips for retail business owners) and share within my networks.
- [ ] Post 1 blog article per week.
- [ ] Post once per day, 6 days per week on Facebook and Instagram, using metrics from each regarding best times to post. Share a combination of images, articles, and tips.
- [ ] Hire graphic designer to work per diem and have first project be direct mail postcard and include an offer for a free, 30-minute consultation. Send out after there is sufficient content on social platforms and website so that potential client can read through blog articles and download free content. Ideally send this during month #3.
- [ ] Post 1 video per week on Wednesday mornings and create a "topic of the week." Share on all platforms.
- [ ] Have graphic designer create share post templates that can be used for 3 months, with a new set for following 3 months.

As you can see from this list, the idea is to look at various to-do tasks to carry out over the next six months, including having a schedule for these tasks. You can go one step further and build this out on a calendar (online or paper). I use Google Calendar, which contains several sub-calendars, one of which I've labeled "Marketing Calendar." I use it to map out all of my marketing plan to-dos and deadlines, and even set reminders.

There are many ways you can organize your marketing plan into a marketing calendar. You can also use project management software. I use both, as I like to use the software to create my to-do items and keep track of ideas or progress I'm making. I like Kanban boards to keep track of what I need to do and what

I've already accomplished, whereas calendars are good for creating a schedule for your list of tasks and helping you stay on schedule.

Software options to help you with your marketing efforts are plentiful and include organizational tools, project management software, customer relationship management (CRM) software, and content management software (CMS), to name a few. The details of these are outside the scope of this book, but know that there are several tools for small business owners available to you. Take some time to research them, try them out, and find the ones that are right for you and your business.

I've discussed stating a goal, giving it a time line, and creating an action plan with to-do items to accomplish the goal. The last piece is to maintain accountability by tracking your progress and confirming that you've met your goal.

For example, after you have gone through all of these items and implemented the plan for three months, ask yourself if you've had any progress. Did you get a single phone call from the direct mail postcard? Are you tracking your followers on social media and seeing an increase? Have you signed any new clients?

Seeing results from marketing plans takes time, but you should see small steps of progress along the way, and you should certainly be able to measure something halfway through the plan. If not, you may want to re-evaluate your plan and see if you need to make any adjustments.

Perhaps you got five phone calls from your direct mail campaign and converted two of them into clients, but you've seen no progress from your networking events, and no one ever emailed you back! You might take from this that investing in a direct mail campaign four times a year could be a good investment, and perhaps in-person networking events should be reduced to once per month or once every two months.

You can hopefully see why you will be much more effective with your marketing efforts if you take the time to create a plan. Without a plan, your marketing isn't focused, quantifiable, or measurable; it doesn't create desired results; and it adds a lot of unnecessary stress. However, with a plan, you can give yourself specific instructions for what to do and when to do it, and you can connect your daily actions with expected result, and measure these results. You can also relax a bit more, because you simply need to follow the plan, rather than wake up each day wondering what you should do to get attention.

Now that you understand the basics of a marketing plan, let's look at one of the main vehicles of marketing: social media platforms.

SOCIAL MEDIA PLATFORMS

If you're like most business owners, you are thinking a big part of your "where" is going to be social media. This may or may not be true, depending on your business, but for most of you, it will play an important role. However, it might not be the role you think. This section breaks down the specifics of these platforms, what you can get from them, and what you should ignore.

Let's debunk a few myths about social media.

MYTH #1: I need to be constantly active on social media to get business.

While this might be true for certain businesses, it isn't true for all businesses. Many business owners get new business through referrals and in-person networking, and online activity is just a piece of earning new business. For social media to be effective, it should be thoughtful, genuine, and strategic. This can be accomplished by focusing more on quality instead of quantity.

Create a social media plan that allows you to schedule your times of being online, and will also include a strategy of what to post, when to post, and why you should post that specific piece of content. Outside of these scheduled times, focus on your business and remove the distractions of social media.

TRUTH #1: Use social media to *engage* with your audience.

It is difficult to get attention for your business online when no one likes to be sold to. Posting what you have to sell all of the time and asking for business will get you nowhere—unless there is something in it for them that they want.

Suppose you sell all-natural, organic, vegan, beauty products. It completely makes sense to use your social media account to show photos of your products, make announcements of new products on the market, and share your story about why you sell organic beauty products. People are looking for these products and they are hard to find. If your audience feels a connection to your story, and your purpose for creating your products, they will feel engaged. Eventually, this might lead to sales.

But even if this is your business, you need to be very strategic about how you use social media to share your story and showcase your products.

<u>Rule #1: Don't just share and walk away!</u> You need to follow other businesses and people, comment, and engage in conversation. Make it about *them* and not you. The best way to do that is to comment on others' content, not just share your own.

<u>Rule #2: Don't just "like."</u> It's easy to go through your feed and click "like," "like," "like" everywhere, but this isn't going to show your audience that you really care. It will just show that you are maybe a little bit interested in them and simply want to give them a high-five in the quickest, easiest way possible. You're better off being selective in who you pay attention to, and engaging in conversation and commenting, rather than just clicking "like" everywhere.

<u>Rule #3: Give!</u> You want to *give.* Give value, give attention, give your interest in others, all of which will make them interested in *you*—and then choose to seek you out and learn more about you.

Make sure that what you give is valuable. Don't just post for the sake of posting or to get attention. Be thoughtful about what you post, and only share what you think is worthy of sharing and will bring value to others. Think quality over quantity, but while being consistent.

MYTH #2: Sharing a lot of content is the only way I'll get noticed.

Sharing too much content can actually turn people away. They'll see your 10th post of the day and think, "Ugh, again? I want to see something else in my feed!" Continue to flood their feed, and they will most likely hide you or unfollow you altogether.

TRUTH #2: Share good content and be consistent.

It's not about sharing a ton of content; it's about sharing good content and being consistent. Setting aside 15 minutes a day to go online and share one worthwhile post is adequate. Stay away from all the cliché quotes and selfies, and post something interesting that your market wants to see. You will create brand awareness in a non-intrusive and helpful way.

MYTH #3: I need to be on every platform.

Every platform has a different group of people and appeals to a different market. Granted there may be reasons to have a *profile* on each—and maybe even use them all from time to time. However, have you noticed how some people post on Facebook, then post the same thing on Instagram, then on Twitter, and once again on LinkedIn? When you see the same post four times, what do you think?

First of all, you should start to wonder why you bother with all four platforms if you're going to see the same information on each. You're also probably going to feel the same way you did experiencing myth #2 (being bombarded by too much content from the same source).

Aside from the idea of sharing the same post four times, it is important to note that while most people are currently on several platforms, they don't necessarily use all of them actively. Most people tend to have a preference of one or two, based on what resonates best with their interests. LinkedIn may be preferred by someone looking for strictly business content, while someone else might prefer Instagram for its focus on lifestyle and visual appeal.

TRUTH #3: Be strategic and choose the platform(s) your customers use.

When I first starting taking clients, I would look for them on LinkedIn to connect. Since LinkedIn is a professional network, and not personal like Facebook, I thought it made sense to connect with everyone I work with on the platform. I would also go to connect on LinkedIn whenever I met someone at a networking event or conference.

Much to my surprise, I found that essentially none of my clients are on LinkedIn. At first I thought, "Why aren't they here?? They run a business, they should be here! Maybe I should tell them to set up an account." But then I realized they had deliberately chosen not to be on LinkedIn for a reason: Simply, it's not where they do business.

Many of my clients are in the B2C world. Their clients and customers are consumers, looking for consumer services and products in industries such as beauty, health, clothing, food, weddings, and wellness, to name a few. LinkedIn is primarily a professional platform on which you would find attorneys, accountants, and other professional services, as well as corporate executives. The posts shared or promoted on LinkedIn tend to be articles from places like *Inc. Magazine,* Bloomberg Business, Entrepreneur.com, and *Forbes.*

This content, and the people using and sharing it, are not really in sync with the businesses I listed as my clients. Now, of course, lawyers get married and corporate executives purchase beauty products, but given the content and conversation going on there, LinkedIn isn't a place you would expect someone to be advertising their clump-free mascara.

Each social media platform has a different purpose, and contains a different audience, which is why a fitness studio owner may be out of place on LinkedIn, but have a highly engaging audience on Facebook and Instagram. Those platforms are where her market is.

In basic terms, if you are in a B2B business, or your client base consists of primarily 9–5 business professionals, then LinkedIn should be your go-to platform. If you're a B2C business, and especially if you sell services and products that vie for disposable income, Facebook or Instagram would work. If you're looking more for quick conversation, rather than CTA (call to action), perhaps Twitter. (However, sharing blog articles, which is technically part of a CTA, works on Twitter.)

I'm tempted to get into the specifics of these platforms, but honestly, the information will be outdated by next year. I'd rather the overall message be that you need to look at each platform. Identify what makes it different from the rest, who the primary users of the platform are, and where your customers spend the *most* time, and choose to focus your efforts there.

Regarding using multiple platforms, you can do this, of course, but use them differently.

For example, you might use LinkedIn to keep connected with past and current colleagues, get information on popular business trends and topics, and be in the loop regarding upcoming business events. You might use Instagram to engage with your audience, showcasing your products or building an interesting story where they want to follow along, and you might use Facebook to share videos or be a member of groups.

Look at your goals and determine what makes sense for your business, rather than trying to post everything, everywhere. Be strategic, and be intentional.

CHAPTER 9

SALES & NEGOTIATION

I GOT MY FIRST LESSON IN SALES as a small business owner when I was 7 years old selling my arts & crafts door-to-door in my neighborhood. Yes, the entrepreneurial bug hit me early. I would knock on doors, introduce myself, show them my product line, and ask for money. You could say I learned to overcome my fear of sales early on, but the truth is, it took decades to overcome it.

Growing up, I didn't have much money, and it caused me to feel anxious about asking others for money or even talking about money! When I became an adult and had to start selling anything, I pictured every person as being financially strapped. I worried that the person I was selling to couldn't really afford it, but felt pressured to buy from me because they either didn't want to hurt my feelings or felt embarrassed to admit they couldn't afford it. I never wanted to make anyone feel that way, so I hated sales and always tried to avoid it.

I eventually hired a coach to help me with this. I learned that I was rocking the sales process, but as soon as I got to the part where I had to ask for the sale, I fell apart. I lost my confidence as well as any chance of closing a deal.

My coach was confused. He knew that I should be awesome at sales, due to my listening skills, authenticity, engaging personality, knowledge of what I was selling, and empathy for the customer, but couldn't understand why I lost my groove at the close. Hearing someone else tell me I had what it takes to be good at sales, but needed to address this one piece, made me realize it was time to overcome my limiting beliefs and open up to the possibility of me being amazing at sales.

If you're an entrepreneur, you're a salesperson. Period. So if you feel like you just can't do sales, you're wrong. Sales is a skill you learn. And like any skill, you don't just learn how to do it. You gain an understanding of it, and you learn how to perform it using your individual strengths.

If you are like many small business owners, you may struggle with sales because you feel you lack the training or the background in it. You probably started your businesses because you wanted to make a living doing something you care about, and your least favorite part of the job is the selling (or maybe tied for first place with keeping track of your finances).

Part of the reason sales is so intimidating is because we often associate it with how we feel when someone tries to sell something to us (especially when it's something we don't want): uncomfortable. Perhaps an even bigger reason is our fear that the person we're asking will no longer like us, or will think differently of us, because we tried to sell to them.

It's important to understand the difference between pushing an unwanted product onto someone and sharing your offerings with someone because you truly believe it will help them. In reality, we sell all the time, and we do it from a place of passion, caring for others, and wanting to help.

When you tell everyone how amazing a new restaurant is and why they must try it, or a friend has told you 10 times how much she loves her new mascara and why you have to buy it, or your brother tells you about a Netflix show that is so funny, you need to start watching it—this is all sales. You sell every time you share your opinion about something you enjoy, with the hope that the person you are talking with will also benefit from it if they try it.

My point is that you have nothing to fear in sales. Your friend won't stop liking you because you tried to convince her your mascara is the best, any more than a sales lead will, as long as your approach is from a good place: passion, caring for others, or wanting to help.

Telling you that you have nothing to fear, though, isn't enough. You need a strategy.

Like many of you, I read books, watched sales presentations, and observed successful salespeople to gain all the insight I could to become a better salesperson. I made note of people who appeared to use unethical tactics and immediately told myself not to follow their advice, then noticed people who were genuine and caring, while also being successful, and gained insight from them. Finally, and perhaps most important, I learned that sales can be an effective way to *help people,* which is really what I aim to do. Over time, I learned strategies that work, ones that don't, and how to feel comfortable selling.

LEARN HOW TO SELL

What are the skills needed in order to be successful at sales and feel comfortable doing it? Here are some of the principles I've learned along the way to help get you started.

- Sales *isn't* about you or your product. It's about the customer—what they want and what they need.
- The sales process should have one goal: to create a mutually beneficial transaction in which the customer feels they gain more than you do, though in reality you're both happy with the result.
- Your job is to solve the customer's problem. You do this by listening attentively, gaining an understanding of their problem, and determining how you and your offerings can solve it.
- You should spend at least 80% of the time listening, and not talking. Giving people the opportunity to share their thoughts, feelings, and

story, and demonstrating that you hear and understand them, is one of the greatest ways to earn business.

- Sales is a discovery process, almost like dating; the purpose is to get to know each other and then determine if you are a good fit. Don't go into a sales meeting simply trying to make a sale. Instead, look to learn from it and discover if a match is made. If it is, the sale is easy; and if it isn't, move on.

- You will save yourself money, time, and headaches if you prioritize qualifying your leads. When a potential sale approaches, don't proceed down the sales rabbit hole if you know right away that they aren't going to be a good fit.

- Don't oversell. It's easy to win the sale and then immediately lose it because you thought you needed to give more information than you really did. Give just enough information to answer their questions without going on and on about all the features of your product or service.

- Be prepared! Know your prices and offerings beforehand, and know what you're willing to accept and not accept regarding terms. Many sales meetings involve negotiation. Know ahead of time whether or not there is anything you are willing to negotiate—and if so, what it is and what your bottom-line price is. Don't make these decisions on the fly; you'll most certainly settle for less than what you really want if you do.

- Don't take *no* personally. It's just business. People have various reasons for choosing not to buy something. It could be that they don't see enough value for the price, they don't really need the product or have other priorities for where they spend their funds, they prefer a competitor's product—the list goes on. Occasionally, there could be a personality conflict, but this is a normal part of social life and not worth getting upset over. Don't get emotional about *nos*. Look at them as part of normal business, and move on.

- If you've done your homework, and truly and accurately defined your market, sales will be much easier. Sales becomes more difficult when you get desperate and try to sell to anyone who comes along. This leads me to . . .

- Don't get desperate! This applies to the entire sales process. Never feel desperate that you have to make a sale (even if you really need the cash). Doing so is like sweating fear in front of a lion. They can smell it a mile away. No one will buy from you if you look like you're desperate. Instead they will wonder: *Is this product any good? Why do they need this sale so badly? Clearly no one is buying it, so what's wrong with the product? Why is this person so anxious to sell it? Is this product worth what they're asking, because they aren't confident selling it?*

- Be confident with yourself, your offerings, and the value you provide. Also be confident with your prices. Sell it like you know it's amazing—and worth every penny.

This list shows you some basic principles that can lead to successful, and even easy, sales. There are a few concepts in this list that I would like to dive a little deeper into.

QUALIFY YOUR LEADS

Qualifying your leads is super important and will make your life *much* easier, but it is also scary for the growing small business owner. The idea of saying no to business, when you really need it, can be tough. But in reality, you aren't really saying no to business. Rather, you're saying *no* to spending time, and even money, trying to win someone over who isn't a good fit and will probably not buy from you anyway. And you're saying *yes* to more time focusing on quality leads.

In order to qualify leads, you need to have a list of what you are looking for in a customer, and match leads to the list. Your list is unique to you and your business, and is based on the work you did earlier to define your market. General categories you would find on this list might be spending power/budget, desire/need, resources, time frame, skill level, commitment, value, and so on.

Suppose you sell luxury automobiles, like Maseratis, and someone calls you inquiring about purchasing one. They want to make an appointment with you for a test drive. They tell you they don't have a driver's license, or a job, but they need a car so they can take their grandmother grocery shopping once a week. What would you do?

Clearly this person is not a good fit for the car. You know right away—from this three-minute phone conversation—that this person is not a quality lead and you will be wasting your time setting up an appointment. It would be more helpful if you explained to them that they would be better off purchasing a station wagon for their grandmother's convenience and comfort. It would also be a more economical choice and a safer first vehicle for a new driver. You send them a referral to a great dealership and wish them luck.

By taking this approach, you have been helpful to them *and* have avoided spending resources on an unqualified lead. Here are some helpful tips for qualifying your leads:

1. Ask questions that will help you *disqualify* them more quickly. It's not that you *want* to disqualify leads, but you want to find the fastest route to discovering if they aren't a good fit.

2. If they aren't a good fit, move on and stop wasting time.

3. If they are a good fit, ask yourself if you can help them. If you can, then offer help and convert them into a sale!

4. If you can't help them, refer them to someone who *can*. Don't be afraid to refer them elsewhere if it's really in their best interest. In the end, it will help build your brand and reputation for being smart, honest, and helpful, which can bring you business down the road. I met with someone once who didn't become a client, but recommended me to several others who *did* become clients.

THE 5 ASKS

Now that you have qualified your lead (in fancy marketing jargon, they are now a "sales opportunity"), it's time to convert them into a sale. Depending on your business, industry, and method of doing business, the advice I could give varies. Someone who runs an online clothing store is going to sell very differently than a divorce attorney, so it's hard to say there is one set sales process everyone should follow, at least a detailed one.

After several years as a business strategist and consultant, working with many clients in service-based industries that involve meeting with potential clients, or at the very least having discovery calls, I created a sales process I call the "5 Asks." When I first started out in my business, my knowledge and expertise didn't close sales for me because my sales process was undeveloped, at best. It wasn't until I created the 5 Asks that I suddenly saw a drastic shift in my sales and started converting nearly every opportunity into a sale.

The 5 Asks is not "salesy," fake, or cliché. It is based on the foundation that I desire to help others as best as I can, with empathy, understanding, and a drive to see them succeed, while also making a living doing what I love.

Note: This is not to be followed to the letter of the law, and each person and conversation are different. It is merely a guide for you to use and incorporate your own charm, personality, and style into. Whether you are on a sales call or meeting with a potential client, follow these steps to build a connection between you and them.

Sell authentically, sell with empathy, and sell with the desire to help.

1. **Ask her to share her story.**

   Start by asking her to share her story. Let her tell you all about her needs, her wants, and what she is hoping to achieve. This gives her the chance to open up about what matters to her and begin to build a connection between you, as well as begin to build trust.

2. **Ask specific questions about her story.**

   Once you have listened to her story, ask specific questions about her story. Use this opportunity to dig deeper and gain a thorough understanding of what she needs, and what her greatest challenges and concerns are. This demonstrates your ability to listen, but, even more important, will let her know she is being heard. It will also help guide the direction of the conversation and what you should be focusing on in order to be the most effective at helping her.

3. **Ask what her desired result is.**

   After she has had the opportunity to share her story, and you've gathered as much background information as needed, ask her what her desired result is. Asking this question will help her articulate her goals and gain her own understanding of what she really wants.

   This is an interesting question to ask, because oftentimes people know they need help, or that they want something better that what they currently have, but they don't know exactly what they want. When you ask this question, it makes them think about this, and actually helps them make an insightful discovery.

4. **Ask how you can help her.**

   Asking this question gives her the chance to tell you exactly what she needs from *you* and creates an image in her mind of how you or your products/services can help her. Once she sees this image, she begins to picture what it's like to use your products or services, or work with you. It also allows you to understand how you can be the most helpful to her—in other words, what you should offer her.

5. **Ask if she would like to get started.**

   This is the big question. It's bold, and it requires a direct answer. It is also the first, and only, time you are asking a *yes* or *no* question. This question is the final qualifier. It is the place where you find out if she is interested or not interested.

IMPORTANT! If she isn't interested, ask, "Why?" Try to find out what the problems or obstacles are, and see if you can address them and even alleviate them. She may, in fact, be interested but struggling to overcome a concern. Your job is to problem-solve and see if you can make it work.

If she still isn't interested, it's time to move on. Offer to follow up with her (and don't forget to do this, which we'll talk more about in the section on follow-up later in this chapter), and let her know that you will be available if questions come up or she becomes interested in the future.

If she isn't interested, it's best not to be pushy. Even if you're anxious to make the sale, don't let that show. Be very matter-of-fact about the whole thing and move on to the next lead. Be confident, and know that leads and opportunities will come and go.

If she *is* interested and seems excited to get started . . .

6. **Make your offer.**

   This is where you finally get to talk! Don't overdo it, though. This is where you bring the 5 Asks together. Recap what she needs, what she wants as her desired result, and how you can help her. Share with her your offering and ask her what she thinks. (I guess you can say this is one more ask.)

Your type of business and your price point will probably determine whether you get an immediate response or if she would like some time to think about it first. If she says, "Sign me up!" that's great, but it may not happen that way most of the time. Tell her to think about it (if she says that is her choice), and that you will follow up with her tomorrow, within the next few days, or by the end of the week (whichever makes the most sense for your business). I would never let an opportunity go more than a week.

If she is truly interested and excited to purchase your product or buy your service, she'll want to do it right away. At the very least, she'll say something like "I definitely want to do this, let me just check on blah, blah, blah first." This might mean she needs to move some money around, talk to a friend or business partner, or something along those lines. Sometimes she will even be the one to give you a follow-up by saying something like "I'm almost positive I'm going to buy this from you. I'll give you a definite answer by tomorrow!" If you don't close the sale that day, one of these two responses is your next best thing.

Be patient. Depending on what you sell and the price tag that comes with it, people may need some time to think about it first. Give them that time, happily.

THE FOLLOW-UP

Ah, the follow-up . . .

This can be tricky because you don't want to follow up too soon, as you risk looking desperate, but if you wait too long, it can cost you the sale. The timing needs to be just right.

So how much time is right?

Well, it really depends on what you are selling, and surprisingly it is not always a matter of cost.

What's the urgency? Are you selling something for which time is of the essence? If so, a shorter follow-up time is necessary. Unfortunately, this isn't something I can tell you without knowing your specific business, but an average would be three to seven days. Anything greater than a week is too long.

How do you approach the follow-up?

Again, you don't want to seem pushy. Keep in mind, though, that the follow-up is meant to give you closure—a *yes* or *no* answer. The smart way to do this is to say something like this:

Hi, Susie.

It was great meeting with you the other day. I really enjoyed hearing your story and learning more about your need to ________________.

I wanted to follow up and see if you have made a decision about whether or not you would like to move forward with ______________________, or if I can answer any other questions you might have.

Look forward to hearing from you.

Kim

Notice a few things about this email letter:

- ❑ It starts by restating her needs.
- ❑ Then it gets directly to the point: Are you interested? No need for fluff here.
- ❑ It concludes by offering to answer any further questions and then stating you want to hear from her. This lets her know you would like an answer, one way or the other.

This is simple and to the point, and it asks for a response. Why do you want to do this? A great salesperson I used to work with said it best: "Kim, your job is to get them to the *no* as fast as you can."

The same principle we discussed in the Qualify Your Leads section applies here. If people aren't interested, you want them to say it, so you can move on to the ones who will say *yes!*

Should you follow up a second time?

Here's my long answer to that: *no!*

Take the hint. If they love you, and want to buy from you, they will. If they don't answer and don't respond to your messages, then they aren't interested. Accept it and move on.

Have confidence in what you sell, and don't waste time begging for business. You're worth more than that.

CALL OR EMAIL?

Again, it depends. Phone calls are definitely more personal and could show that you are really interested in being helpful, but they can also feel intrusive. Most people, me included, are not fans of the phone ringing, especially if the person on the other end wants money. However, if you feel that the relationship is close enough that it warrants a personal phone call, then go for it. Otherwise, you should probably stick to the written word and send an email.

A few good things about email are that it's less intrusive, and your thoughts are clear and to the point. Email also gives the recipient time to think about responding and what they want to say, if anything, and also gives them the chance to ignore your message if they aren't interested. The downside is you may be wondering for a few days if they are going to get back to you, whereas if you called you'd have your answer right away.

Note that many books on sales say the opposite and encourage you to *not* give the person a chance to say no or to ignore you. I disagree. You're there to help, not just close a deal, and you should have their interests at heart. This means not wanting to swindle them into a quick decision they aren't ready to make. If someone decides to work with me, I want them to really want to work with me! I don't want them to decide under pressure and later regret they said *yes* before they were ready to commit.

We all have a different style. Do whatever feels more comfortable to you.

CAN YOU CHANGE THEIR MIND?

The short answer to this is *maybe.* Before you can know the true answer, you need to find out *why* they aren't interested. Does it have anything to do with you or your product, or is it for reasons that have nothing to do with either and are out of your control?

When you sell to others, there is much more present in the situation than you, them, and the product: their attitude toward money, their spending or saving habits, their level of confidence in their own ability to make good decisions, their perception of need vs. want, their preconceptions about you or your product (which may not be real or accurate but are based on previous experiences they've had with similar products or people), and much more. While you can't change the external factors, you can dig deeper to find out what is really holding them back from purchasing from you. Perhaps you can address these issues, help them overcome their objections, and change their mind.

For example, suppose you are selling beauty products and the person you are selling to has had several bad experiences with other makeup lines in the past. They've spent hundreds of dollars on products that they wound up not liking or not using, or, worse, that caused bad skin reactions. Over time, they have learned to not trust the uncertainty that comes with buying new lines of makeup and skincare products, in fear they are throwing away money.

If you are honest, and confront them about what is keeping them from purchasing, and encourage them to be honest with you, they may share this fear with you. They will also tell you that because of this fear, they are not going to buy from you. Rather than walking away, you can take this opportunity to empathize with their situation, and determine if you can alleviate their fears and offer a solution to their problem.

In this situation, offering a money-back guarantee if they don't like the products could turn a *no* into a *yes.* You could also offer to sell them just one product and see if they like it, telling them they can always buy more later if they like this first product. Your particular product, service, and situation will determine how you can address their fears.

Your job is not to turn a *no* into a *yes* if it is a true *no.* Your job is to figure out if a *no* isn't really a *no,* but a *maybe.* Make sense?

Being good at sales means being empathetic and being a problem-solver. Understand your prospect, try to find their problems ("pain points" in sales terms), and determine if what you offer can fix their problems. If it can, you need to be able to communicate this and get the prospect to understand how you can alleviate their pain.

Keep in mind that they might not always be aware, or be able to articulate, what their pain is. They might need you to articulate it for them. Show them you are listening by taking what you've heard and repeating it back to them in a way that clearly explains their problem, followed by letting them know you can provide a solution. For example, suppose you are a business coach, and a client tells you how they never have enough time to get their projects completed and they are completely stressed. They may perceive their problem as not having enough time and are looking to you for help with time management. However, you might realize that their problem isn't time, but rather that they need to hire help and delegate more.

Aside from solving problems, you can also show them the intangible benefits you bring them. Your expertise, experience, and knowledge can save them time, alleviate stress, and provide a sense of comfort and assurance that their needs are being met. For example, if you're a website developer and your prospect needs to create an e-commerce site with payment processing, inventory tracking, and a reliable CRM, you already know the programs, plugins, and platform to use, and can easily create the site with all the desired functionality in a short amount of time. However, your prospect could spend weeks, if not months, trying to figure it all out, and the end result may still not be what they want.

If you can successfully show your prospect how you can solve their problems, and show them how they will benefit from buying from you, you will have a much greater chance of earning new business and hearing more prospects say *yes!*

NEGOTIATE LIKE NOBODY'S BUSINESS (LIKE A BOSS)

"No, you take the last slice of pizza. I insist! Yes, I know I haven't eaten yet today, but you're hungry, right? I'll eat later. It's totally fine. No, seriously, you have the pizza!"

Does this sound like you?

Always wanting to give to others usually goes along with not wanting to ask for anything for yourself. Honestly, as I sit here and write, I'm trying to think of times in my younger days where I asked for something I wanted, and I'm drawing a blank.

This is why negotiating is so hard: It requires you to actually tell someone else *what you want!* Not only that, but you are saying it to someone who may not want to give it to you *and* who may benefit from you *not getting your way.* Whoa!

First things first: Shake the monkey off your back that whispers in your ear things like "Don't ask for what you want. You'll seem demanding, bossy, greedy, selfish, [fill in the blank]." Or how about "Be grateful you've gotten this far! You're going to lose this deal if you ask for anything . . ."?

You have every right to advocate for yourself, your wants, your needs, and for what you truly think is fair. Say this to yourself over and over again until it sinks in. Remember: No one—and I mean *no one*—is going to fight for you. You need to fight for yourself. So get in that ring, throw on the gloves, and get ready to negotiate like a boss!

Once I started business consulting, I quickly realized that I am pretty good at coaching others—knowing what they should do and how they should do it. And it came so easy to me. Why? Because I wasn't the one who had to do it. It is always easier to give someone else advice than to do anything ourselves.

I had clients in situations in which they needed to negotiate, whether it be contracts, leases, business transactions, new client deals, or new employee agreements. I was the cheerleader telling them how to negotiate, ask for what they want, and not settle. Everything I taught them I learned by reading books and doing research on the topic, but my first experience putting it all into practice was by coaching my clients on how to negotiate and watching what happened in the aftermath.

You'll be happy to hear that it worked, and my clients were thrilled with the results of their newly acquired negotiating skills. Since then, I have had plenty of opportunities to negotiate for myself and put into practice all the techniques I taught my clients at the beginning of my business.

Here are my negotiation tips:

1. Never make the first offer. Let the other person offer first. For example, suppose you are negotiating the terms of a business agreement in which you and another business owner will be referring clients to each other and offering a referral fee. Don't be the first to suggest a fee rate. Ask them what amount they think is fair. This is only step one, so don't stop here.

2. Exaggerate your counter-offer. Once you have let the other person name their price, you need to counter-offer—but at a price that is higher or lower than what you want. For example, let's say your ideal number is $1,000. You start by letting the other person name their price. Let's assume they say $800. Rather than countering at $1,000, counter at $1,200. This will force them to go up to $900. You counter at $1,100, they counter at $1,000, and you agree to that price. You have made the other person feel as if it is a compromise, and that they were in control, but you got exactly what you wanted.

3. Know what you want from the deal. This could be your ideal price, or ideal results, or something else. Just make sure you are clear on what you want. You may not get exactly what you want, and you probably won't, but you need to know three things: what you want ideally, what you're willing to settle on and still be happy, and what is *not* acceptable to you. As you enter the negotiation process, aim for your ideal, be willing to compromise on your settle (again, should still be something that makes you happy), and be willing to say *no* to what you don't want and even walk away if your minimum requirements aren't met. If you don't know these three things before entering the negotiation, you will most certainly settle for what you don't want. And *never* be or act desperate.

4. Remember: It isn't all about you. While you should use these negotiations to get what you want and advocate for yourself, you must remember that it isn't all about you. The other person also wants what they want, and to make you both happy, a compromise will need to be made and you will need to be cognizant of their point of view.

The examples here have to do with negotiating price or money, but you can use these skills to negotiate anything. Just follow the basic principles of each step, whatever it is you are negotiating.

CHAPTER 10

MAXIMIZE YOUR RESOURCES

RESOURCES ARE THE TOOLS YOU HAVE OR NEED to grow your business. These resources include your skills, experience, and education, as well as your network and funds, but they also include what others have that you need to acquire. Ask yourself what you can contribute, as well as who you need to hire or bring on board, in order to grow your business.

ASSESS YOUR SKILLS

Up to this point, the conversation about what you sell, how you sell it, and to whom you sell has been all about you and your perception of your brand, company, and market. It's time to branch out and start looking at who is on your team, what resources you have, both internally within the company and externally, and how can you best leverage what you have to get maximum results.

But before we seek outside help, let's look at *you* and what you bring to the table. Each of us has strengths and weaknesses, traits that make us successful and traits that are sometimes a hindrance. As a smart and savvy business owner, you need to identify the skills and traits you possess and those traits and skills you lack (and need to find elsewhere) that, combined, will lead your business on the path to greatness.

This is an easier task for some than others. For example, I am pretty confident, and I have no problem telling people what I'm good at and what I'm not good at. Numbers would be a yes; singing would be a no. (This doesn't stop me from occasionally daydreaming that I'm a rock star, but I clearly know I shouldn't quit my day job.)

Have an open and honest conversation with you, yourself, and your make-believe microphone, and nail down a list of your skills and need-to-acquire skills. Don't judge; just be pragmatic. Look at this exercise as nothing more than a business exercise—because that is all it is.

It's okay to admit that you're not great at everything *and* that you may actually not be great at all the detailed business skills, such as accounting or technology. Many small business owners don't have any business skills until they go into business and learn them on the job! It's your passion that led you to start a business, not your desire to be an expert in business. However, in order for your business to grow, you need to move past just being passionate, and run your business with efficiency and productivity in mind.

As a business owner, your job is to manage a machine. That machine is made up of several small parts that all work together to create an efficient and synergistic system. You oversee all of these parts and make sure everything is working as it should. You understand that when one part starts to fail, it impacts the entire machine and it needs to be fixed. However, you're not one of the parts, and you don't need to do the job of the parts. Make sense?

I use this example to illustrate that you don't *have* to be good at all of the components of your business. You only need to know *what you need* and *how to get it.* So let's start by looking at what you *have.*

Make a list of your skills—things you're good at. If you want to be really detailed, divide them into two categories: hard skills and soft skills. In a nutshell, hard skills are skills that are easily teachable, school-oriented subjects—things like math, statistics, and writing. Soft skills are those that are hard to teach, but may be developed with the right instruction, such as leadership skills, self-awareness, negotiation skills, and having patience.

After you have made your list of all the things you're good at, think about the skills you may not have, but think you need to run your business successfully. For example, you might be aware that you are a good writer (a hard skill), but you are not strong with technology. This will give you the opportunity to recognize that you shouldn't be wasting your time trying to figure out all of the software you need for your business, and instead should hire someone else to do that for you.

This exercise should be something that takes some thought and time. Sit down, get comfortable, grab yourself a notebook and a pen, and start identifying what you have, what you lack, and who can help you get it. As you work on this exercise, you start with a simple skills list, but let this evolve into thinking about the different parts of your business and where you need help. It should also help you decide the best way for you to use your skills to grow your business.

For example, if you are a great writer, use this to guide marketing content, and if you outsource your content writing, use your skill to guide the writer on what you want your message to be. If you are highly organized, use that to help you create an overall business plan, team chart, and project management system. If you're not good at being organized, hire someone to organize your business and projects for you.

You can create a Skills Chart similar to the following example.

SKILLS CHART

Skill I Have	How can I use it?
Artistic	Create branded and well-designed social media share templates Design decor and choose gift items for events
Social	Network and find new clients Speak at events; lead workshops and classes
Creative	Create content such as online videos and courses

Skill I Need	Where can I get it?
Financial	Hire a part-time bookkeeper
Organizational	Hire an independent contractor to set up project management system
Technical	Hire web developer to create website with shopping cart integration

Assuming you are in the early stages of your business (and the fact that you bought this book tells me this is likely), you may not yet be in a financial position to delegate to a dozen people. If so, this exercise can be extremely helpful to you because as you bootstrap your company, as most of us have had to do, you *will* need to do a lot yourself in the beginning. Use this exercise to figure out what you are really great at, so you don't need to hire out right away for everything, but also to determine what should be your first priority when you are ready to start bringing people in.

DIY VS. HIRING

That being said, you need to hire much earlier than you think. I'm going to repeat that: You need to hire much earlier than you think!

Many small business owners hesitate to start bringing in outside resources. This could include hiring people like attorneys, accountants, bookkeepers, graphic designers, social media managers, content writers, administrative assistants, and so on. This is a big mistake. People who refuse to hire, or refuse to invest in their businesses, are like fish swimming in a shallow pool of water, gasping for air. They struggle and struggle, and never get ahead.

Here's the hard truth: You can't build a business by yourself. You can't. You cannot succeed or grow your business to the point where you are living your ideal life if you stay in your silo, insist on doing everything yourself, and refuse to part with money. If you do this, you will be like our suffocating fish. You will continue to struggle and work 10 times harder than you need to, and you won't get the results you need any time soon, or ever.

You must find people who are great at what they do, invest in them, and let them build your business. Hire people who are smart, talented, and experts in their fields, and trust them to take your business to the next level. This could be something as small as hiring a graphic designer to do all of your social media posts, or a slightly higher commitment of hiring an assistant to help you get organized and free up your time so you can focus on bringing in sales.

If you are doing too much work yourself, you are drowning in mundane tasks that get you nowhere—and generate zero dollars. If you need customers, go out and get them. Let someone else do the writing, the typing, the post design, the email management. Get, find, borrow the money you need to start building a well-oiled machine.

Hiring people, as long as they are the right people, is an *investment*. This is not the same as *spending*.

This relates to both building your company overall and maximizing the day-to-day revenue.

Here is a simple example. Suppose you earn $250 per hour for client work, but you spend most of your time doing work you don't get paid for (organizing, emailing, marketing, etc.). Every time you use up your day working on non-billable time, you *lose* money. You could hire an assistant for a much lower hourly rate than yours to do this work, thus giving you more time to earn money. The following graphic compares doing the work yourself vs. hiring out to an assistant whose rate is $25 per hour.

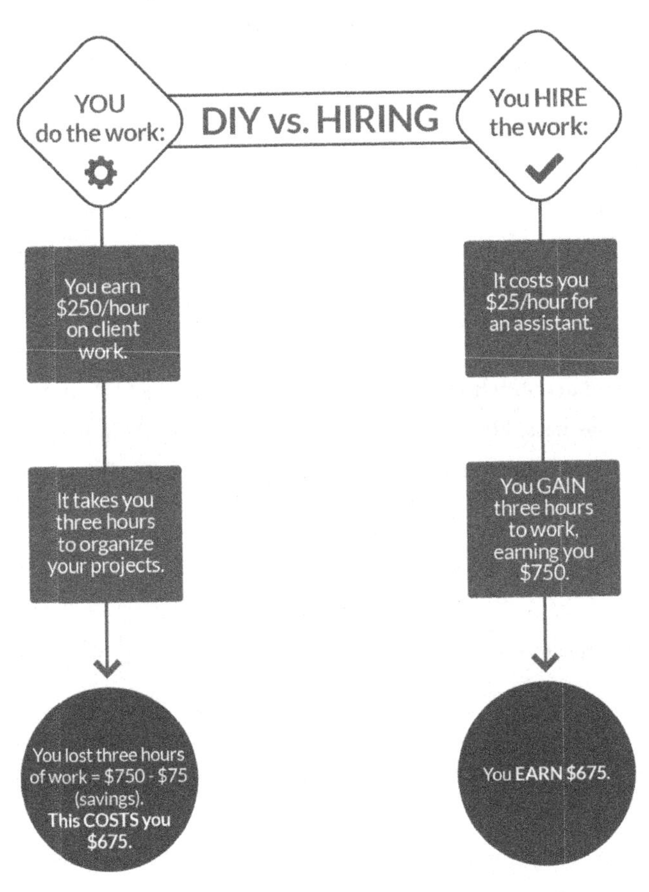

You might be saying to yourself, "Well, Kim, I get this and I agree, but I just started my business and I currently don't have much money coming in. I need customers. So I can't afford to hire anyone yet."

This is even more reason to hire out! You need to be getting customers and making sales, and you can't do that if you're spending all your time building your own website, doing all of your own graphic design, setting up client software, and all the other tasks you're doing that don't generate sales. When you do this, you are postponing getting customers and making money!

Here comes a truth you may not want to hear: You have to invest in your business *before* you have the money to do so. You need to believe that your business will work before it actually works, and have faith that, if you invest money today, tomorrow you will be successful.

This leads me to ask: Do you *believe* in your business? Do you believe it can work? If you do, then investing money today shouldn't feel like such a risk. If you don't, ask yourself why not.

Just to be clear, I'm not suggesting you max out your credit cards to hire everyone you can think of. Be smart about your finances and know what it makes sense to invest in, to give you faster, greater returns on your investment and make progress in growing your business. For example, refer to the Skills Chart, specifically where you recognize it would be better to hire a bookkeeper. Suppose you earn $200 per hour for your services, and you can pay a bookkeeper $35 per hour. It is wise to invest in hiring a bookkeeper rather than doing the work yourself. It's better to pay someone $35 so that you can earn $200 than it is to spend that time saving $35 but not earning anything.

There are people who do everything themselves, incur no debt of any kind, and slowly build their businesses. This technically works, but could take several years just to get to the point of barely getting by. If you are smart from the beginning, and look for ways to invest in your business, growing your business can be less stressful and happen much quicker.

When delegating and hiring, don't be afraid to pay for quality and don't fear hiring employees (more on this later).

Let's start with the first point: pay for quality. Often new business owners let price dictate who they hire. This leads them to hiring "the friend of a friend" who does this work on the side, is new themselves, and is super cheap—but is also very inexperienced. They wind up paying money, which at this point they have very little of, for work that isn't worth anything, thus wasting their money and resources.

I see this often when it comes to things like web design, graphic design, marketing/social media managers, and office assistants. I've even seen this with accountants and attorneys.

Business owners wind up with a website that looks awful, logos they bought on a $5 website, or an assistant who can't do anything without being told exactly what to do (and then still mess up and need to be let go eventually because they didn't do anything helpful!).

When money is tight and you're just starting out, you *need* experienced people. You need people who will lift you up and help you grow your business; to do this, they can't be newbies too. Decide what is most important to your business and invest in it. It could be having a nice website done, especially if you are planning to use it to sell online, or hiring a talented graphic designer (remember: They help you build your brand), an excellent photographer, or an assistant who can practically run your business without you showing up!

So when you're looking for help, the going rate for assistants is $25–35 per hour, and your "friend" tells you they can recommend someone who's so-and-so's college-aged daughter and she'll do it for $12 an hour, politely say, "No, thanks." (And think to yourself, "*No way!*") Look for the person who can do the job and do it well, is someone you feel you can trust, and impresses you so much, you think they know more than you.

You might be thinking that this all sounds well and good, but wondering how you will pay for it. Everyone's situation is different, but here are some things I see:

- ❑ Some people have family or friends willing to loan them a few dollars to help them start or invest in their business.
- ❑ Others rely on credit or loans.
- ❑ A few use crowdfunding sites where they can pitch to everyone they know to support their projects.

- ❑ Don't quit your day job just yet, and build up some savings that you set aside specifically for business growth.

When people want something enough, they find the money. It's all about priorities. I've seen people state they have no money to invest in their business, but then vacation to Hawaii or the Caribbean, or walk around with their Coach handbag while eating sushi and drinking $10 raw juices every day. They *do* have the money; they simply choose where to spend it, and where not to spend it. In this example they chose to spend it rather than invest it.

If you want to build your business the right way, be willing to invest money before spending it. If you invest in your business today, you will grow it to the point where you will eventually have plenty of money to spend on all the niceties you want. This mindset is so important if you want to succeed. You must go from living in the moment, to planning ahead for the future. Invest, invest, *invest!*

BUILD YOUR TEAM: CONTRACTORS

We've established that as you build a team to support you and your business, you will have more time and resources to focus on growth. The way you build that team varies based on your business, though. Solopreneurs are less likely to need a team of employees, but primarily need an external support team, typically made up of independent contractors (ICs). This includes a long list of people you can call upon when you need certain tasks done on a per diem basis. Web developers, graphic designers, content/copywriters, attorneys, and accountants are among those on this list.

You also will most likely need one or more ICs as ongoing contractors. This could include virtual/office assistants, social media managers, or bookkeepers. These people may have businesses of their own, and you are one of their clients, rather than them being your employee.

There are many benefits to this arrangement for small business owners, especially those in service-based industries. You can have access to several, if not a dozen, different services without having to worry about hiring part-time or full-time employees for each service you need, making this a cost-effective method to get the resources you need.

Finding ICs is very different from hiring employees. ICs can typically be found through your network and are often referrals. This is preferable, because you want those you know and trust to recommend them. For example, if you needed a copywriter for marketing material and someone you know hired a copywriter they thought did an amazing job, you're more likely to hire that person based on the recommendation. ICs are also already in the B2B space and therefore can be found through networking events, online communities, and social media.

If you find someone online for whom you didn't get a referral, make sure you get references, ask to see their portfolio, and search their business online to see if you can find reviews or any press about them. However, even with a referral it is a good idea to do your homework and research before hiring.

If you are looking for someone to help you, it is also a good idea to get multiple referrals and interview a few people before deciding who to hire. This is especially true for contractors you plan to work with for a long time, or for expensive projects like web design.

You begin the process of hiring typically through emails and/or phone calls to confirm that the person you wish to hire is a good fit and can perform the services that you need. Once a verbal agreement is made, the IC will usually provide you with a contract. (They typically have a standard contract for all of their clients to sign.) That contract should detail the expected services to be provided, the time frame in which the work will be performed, as well as payment amounts and terms. There may be times when the person doing the hiring might present the contract, as well.

While there will be contractors that you hire for a one-time project, ideally you will build a team of consistent contractors with whom you work on a regular basis as you grow your business. For example, when you first start your business you will need to hire a graphic designer to design your logo and branding materials. As you grow, you will continue to have projects requiring design, such as social media templates, website updates, printed materials for in-person business events, online materials for advertising, providing content to prospects—the list goes on.

Building a team of contractors whom you trust and can call upon whenever you have a new project will be extremely helpful to you as you grow your business. Being able to delegate projects that are outside the scope of what you do, to others who specialize in their respective fields, will make your job easier and less stressful, and will give you more time to focus on running your business without getting lost in the tasks. You will also feel confident that your business needs are being met by qualified professionals.

One final note: While ICs are not employees, there are still tax issues to consider when hiring ICs. You may be required to issue a 1099 form at the end of the year to your ICs if they meet certain criteria, in which case you will need to provide them with a W-9 form to fill out. A W-9 (Request for Taxpayer Identification Number and Certification) includes the contractors EIN (Employer ID Number) or Social Security number, and is needed to issue a 1099 form. To find out if you are required to issue 1099s to your ICs, consult with your CPA or tax accountant.

BUILD YOUR TEAM: EMPLOYEES

While many small business owners, especially in the online business community, tend to favor working with ICs, there are times when it becomes necessary to hire an employee over a contractor. There are legalities involved that are beyond my scope of expertise, as well as outside the scope of this book, specific to what qualifies someone to be an employee over a contractor. Ask your attorney about the details and/or do some research on your state employment laws. For our purposes we will compare the difference between hiring a contractor who works for you as well as several other clients and is in business for themselves, and hiring an employee who only works for you and is not in business for themselves.

You will most likely find that the first employee you need to hire is an office manager/assistant, a "Jill of All Trades" to whom you can pass off a lot of random administrative tasks, but who you can also rely on to manage projects, keep you organized, and take care of the small stuff—so you can focus on the big stuff.

Once you bring this person on board, the idea is that they will do such an amazing job supporting you that you are able to focus on bringing in business and doing what people pay you for, that you will make enough money to hire more people you need. This could be others who do what you do so you can now take on more clients for the company overall, doubling sales, and then tripling sales, and so on. As you grow, you might replace more of your contractors with employees, building a bigger team with bigger profits.

There's no set path for hiring employees, but you will most likely start with an office manager/assistant and go from there. Your industry, business, and current resources will determine who is next in line to be hired.

For example, if you make and sell products, you will probably want to bring on salespeople early. Hire salespeople who really believe in the company, the products, and the mission, and who spend their time and energy focused on helping you grow the business. When you bring salespeople into a company early on, they tend to feel they are a part of something that matters, members of the team, and often motivated to see your vision come to life.

You will know who you need to hire as the business progresses. It will come from the organic growth of the company as you realize you are lacking help in certain areas, and really need to bring someone on to do these tasks or take over these roles.

The struggle I most often see is that small business owners have so many odds and ends that they need help with that, when added together, don't equal an easily identifiable or describable position. For example, you might need someone to manage your books (a number-crunching finance person) and also to design and send email campaigns (a creative designer and marketer). It is usually tough to find one person who can do both tasks.

This is one of the reasons why outsourcing much of your services in the beginning is the way to go, until your business has grown to the point of having enough work to hire employees. It may be hard to imagine that your small business, generating $250,000 today, could be generating $1,000,000 in the future, and you'll actually have enough work to hire several employees. It all just takes planning and time.

The whole process of having employees seems scary when you've never had them before. The taxes, bookkeeping, payroll, benefits, legal considerations—it all seems overwhelming.

It is much easier than you think. Once you realize that you need to bring in some help and start building your staff, the first things to do are figure out exactly what you need help *with* and put together a list of job duties, a job description, and a job title.

Next, determine how much can you afford to pay them and what the going rate in your area and industry for such a position is. Keep in mind smaller companies don't have the budget that larger companies have, but they usually offer other perks in their place.

Once you have a job title, description, duties, and salary, it's time to figure out where to advertise. My advice is to post the job on your business website and share on social media among your networks. There are several advantages to this. Why? First, your post will be seen by your current fans, who already like you and your company, and who believe in what you're selling. They are also familiar enough to be able to show real interest in an interview. Second, your network has several people you can trust who will share this job with people they know and like, helping to build a worthwhile pool of interested candidates. Third, your network may have people already working in your industry, which means they might be more experienced for the job than someone who is simply looking for a job. Fourth, you'll bring traffic to your website.

Once you receive a few good resumes and inquiries, review them and decide who is worth interviewing. Set up some phone calls, then interviews, until you find the right match. At this point you can write an offer letter or move right to the employment agreement, which I suggest you have an attorney draft for you. Attorneys can create a template that you can use for all your employees, so you don't need to hire them over and over for each new hire.

The employment agreement will have the details such as their job title, duties, description, salary, benefits, pay schedule, vacation schedule, employee reviews schedule, and that they are employees-at-will, meaning they can choose to quit at any time and you can fire them for any reason, as long as you don't violate employment laws, such as discrimination. You and your new employee sign the agreement, and you now have an employee!

Payroll is typically outsourced. A payroll company will take care of all of this for you, including getting your new hire set up and in the payroll system. Outsourced payroll is inexpensive and usually a better choice than trying to take care of it yourself. They'll take care of getting you set up for state and federal payroll taxes, as well as unemployment and Medicare.

You'll also need to have your new employee fill out paperwork for both the company and the government. You can download standard employment from your state labor department as well as the IRS website. Your attorney, accountant, or payroll company should be able to advise you on this as well.

LEVERAGE YOUR NETWORK

One of the strongest resources you have—that often gets overlooked—is your network. When you first go into business for yourself, no one knows you exist unless you tell them. You could create the most beautiful website and business cards, and offer much-needed services or fabulous products, but if you don't tell people about your business, you won't get any business.

Think of a couple of people you know who work in real estate, especially those successful in real estate, and ask them how they got started. I guarantee you they will each give you the same answer: They told all of their friends and family about their new real estate business. They sent emails to everyone they knew letting them know that they are now real estate agents, and stating that if they ever are interested in buying, selling, or renting, to please think of them and reach out. Someone they knew would take them up on the offer and, from there, would make a referral. From there, like branches on a tree, more people in their network were interested, more referrals came in, and the business grew.

However, many other new business owners, outside of industries like real estate, forget to do this. Perhaps people assume their network is made up of people who wouldn't be their customers (so why tell them all?). Even if this may be true, you don't know for sure, but you also don't know your network's network. Maybe the person you know won't be a customer, but someone *they know* will be.

Sending an email to all your contacts, letting them know about your business and asking them to tell others they know who might be interested, is a great way to bring awareness to your business.

Another way to leverage your network is to look for opportunities for collaboration. Create a list of everyone you know who might like to work with you on a project or event, and reach out and ask if they would be interested. For example, using our skincare product line from earlier in the book, you could reach out to people you know who are hair stylists, salon owners, or fashion stylists, and ask if you could host a joint beauty event with them. It could include a "how-to" class where attendees get to sample the products, learn more about clean beauty, and have some appetizers and beverages while networking.

Collaborative events bring many benefits to you and your business. You get to leverage someone else's network, because they are inviting all of their people to be introduced to *you!* This, of course, helps your own network grow. It also increases your credibility when you are being brought in by another person or company, giving you more of an expert reputation. Collaboration can also help you build relationships with others who are more likely to recommend you after they've had a chance to work with you and get to know you better.

Finally, collaborative events also help you get found more online and bring brand awareness. Every time you host an event with someone else, who advertises the event on their website, or sells tickets online, your name is showing up in more places online. Someone searching your name, if they perhaps came across your products or services and wanted to learn more, will now see that you have hosted several events with various other businesses, and this will give you a reputation of being successful and well-established.

For example, suppose you are an interior decorator and you've collaborated with several home furnishing stores in the area. If someone searches your name, they will see you affiliated with all of these different, well-known local furniture shops and assume you *must* be an expert in the field.

A final note about your network: choose wisely. If you build your professional network among people and within a crowd that does not resonate with you, your brand, or your business, you need to get out of it and find a new network. Remember what I said about branding, focusing on your niche market, and weeding out your unqualified leads? All of those principles apply to your network as well.

While you will be the leader for the development of your brand, your brand will also build on its own, outside of your business, and sometimes out of your control. The best example of this is how your brand builds based on other's experiences with your company, and what information they share with the public. It also builds from how others perceive your business.

With our skincare example, suppose your products are high-end products, made with the best of ingredients. Your market and brand are all about luxury skincare, and your goal is to sell your products in the finest spas and salons in major cities throughout the world. However, you decide to get desperate about getting your business out there (remember my thoughts on being desperate!) and you offer to showcase your products at a local salon that is known for being cheap, dirty, and low-end quality.

You get to know the owners of this salon and they refer you to other cheap and low-end salons, and now you are building your network with these types of businesses. When the luxury salons you hope to get into see this, they will immediately assume your products are also cheap and will never want to do business with you.

As you build your network, be mindful of this. Associate yourself and your business with others who match your brand. This will have a great impact on how you are perceived in the marketplace, and will help you build brand awareness, credibility, and reputation among the people you are most trying to reach.

Let's recap this chapter's main points:

1. Make a list of your skills and talents. Decide which ones you can use to help propel your business forward. In the beginning, figure out which of these skills you can leverage as you bootstrap up and need to do most, if not all, of the work yourself.

2. Make a list of the skills you need, but lack. Figure out who has these skills and make a plan to start hiring others to fill in these gaps. This doesn't need to be hiring full-time or even part-time employees, but can simply be independent contractors or service firms.

3. Hire sooner rather than later. Start by hiring for the skills you need most. That will help free up your time the most, so that you can focus on generating sales.

4. Make smart financial decisions when hiring and growing, and make sure anyone you bring on is an investment.

5. Leverage your network. Tell everyone you know about your business, and ask them to tell others.

6. Look for opportunities to collaborate and work with others who align with your brand.

CHAPTER 11

PLAN FOR FUTURE GROWTH

AMONG THE MOST IMPORTANT THINGS you can do for your business are to always be looking ahead and anticipating changes in your industry, market, and competition, as well as having a plan for how you want to grow in relation to these changes.

Most business owners are stuck in the here and now (which I've talked about extensively in this book) and need regular reminding about the importance of focusing on the future. Think about companies that at one point in time were big game-changers and are now obsolete or out of business. Those of us old enough have seen many businesses make their mark as being the place where everyone shopped—and then not survive. My generation (Gen Xers) has seen restaurants, department stores, book stores, music stores, clothing stores—you name it—that were once staples of our childhoods come and go.

Why does this happen? Because these companies didn't think ahead, anticipate change, and have a plan for adapting to change. The world is an ever-changing place, and if you don't work and move with the changes, your business will become irrelevant. Successful business owners are the ones who were able to change their business models along the way to keep up with changing technology, changing trends, and changing consumer demands.

These concepts are just as important for the small business owner who is more volatile and more prone to going out of business than the big, multi-million-dollar stores. Anticipating what might come in the future, being ready for it, and even adapting just slightly earlier than your competition might be the keys to outpacing your competition and continuing to grow a thriving business.

In order to do this, you must stay current on the news, trends, and current events happening within your industry. What new products are coming to market? What new technology will soon be available, and how do you use it? What new competitors will soon be on the scene? Stay ahead of the learning curve and know your industry, market, and changing consumer demands.

I owned a health and wellness business for many years, and from the time I entered the industry until the time I left it, I saw many changes in all of these areas. When I got my first job as a personal fitness trainer and group exercise instructor, there were no phone apps that would allow you to scan a barcode and automatically know all the nutrients in what you just ate, no watches that could calculate your exercise calories, and no blogs that would dispense hundreds of thousands of recipes tailored to meet the needs of any specific diet.

Could you imagine if I were still a nutritionist today and instead of having my clients use these technologies, I was asking them to manually calculate their food intake and keep track of everything in a notebook? Most likely, my clients would think I was a dinosaur and would seek out a health coach who was up to speed with technology and phone apps.

No matter what you do for work, there will be changes in the future. While you can't specifically plan for changes you don't know will happen, you *can* set your business up in a way that allows for change and is open to change.

Like I already mentioned, be in the know about as much as you can. This will come not only by staying current with industry publications and the news, but also seek out opportunities to continuously network with others in your industry, join local clubs and professional organizations, and attend industry-specific conferences, at least once a year.

The more you know about changes in your industry and in market demand, the more you can leverage these to generate new ideas for your business. You might decide to start offering a new service or product, based on what is going on in the market. A great example of this would be the various changes we've seen in the last 15 years in the yoga industry.

When I started teaching group exercise, yoga was something most people didn't do. We were still doing what was called "hi-lo aerobics," kickboxing, and, my personal favorite, step aerobics. (Yep, this was a long time ago!) Yoga studios were rare and seemed to appeal to a small, specific kind of hippie audience. When yoga started to earn some buzz, fitness centers, like the one I worked in, wanted to incorporate yoga with the other fitness classes offered. Pilates was also becoming popular, and, combined with yoga, created a new class called yogalates. Fitness centers and gyms began experimenting with offering yoga in funky classes—in order to follow the trend of yoga becoming more popular with the general population. Following these pop-based yoga classes, fitness centers started offering traditional yoga classes as well. This became a problem for the more authentic yoga studios, because they were now competing with fitness centers.

Think of what happened (and still exists today): Yoga studios, which only offer yoga, were charging membership fees of, say, $75–125 per month. But for just $50 per month, you could join a gym that offered yoga but also had a variety of fitness classes, machines, weights, and maybe even a swimming pool. Yoga studios needed to find a way to stand out and convince the market that what they offered is different from what you can get in a gym.

So what did we see next? Hot yoga. The ability to stand on your head in a room that is cranked to 100 degrees. (That may not be true. I've never really tried it. I just know it's hot in there and people really good at yoga can do headstands.) Hot yoga studios had something gyms couldn't offer without having the headache of changing their HVAC systems to accommodate one or two classes a week.

Next, yoga studios started to collaborate with other holistic health practitioners like acupuncturists, Reiki specialists, and energy healers—all very popular right now. Offering workshops, classes, and retreats on various holistic health and wellness topics has helped build the multi-billion-dollar alternative health industry we see today.

Yoga studios were able to continuously grow and develop because when competition infiltrated their space, they stayed on top of it and adapted to their new environment. They were able to see an opportunity from this competition. What opportunity? The opportunity to differentiate themselves from the fitness industry, and create an entire new movement focused on health and wellness, rather than fitness.

The yoga industry not only leveraged the competition, but also capitalized on the changes happening within the market. Many people, especially women, were feeling frustrated with the fitness industry's promotion of unrealistic expectations. Fitness magazines covered with women in bikinis, unsustainable diets, and a one-size-fits-all approach to fashion, beauty, and weight were coming under scrutiny.

People were yearning for inner peace free from judgment and full of acceptance. They wanted to feel good in their own skin and develop a healthier relationship with their body image and self-worth. This path led many to become interested in the impact of their environment, which led to an interest in living a more authentic and holistic life. The yoga industry took the roots and philosophies of yoga, all about the holistic mindset so many were craving, and incorporated it into their offerings and branding. They aligned themselves with others who shared these views and, together, created a movement that the people so badly wanted.

Twenty years ago yoga studios were few and far between. Look around today; there are yoga studios everywhere. It's a highly competitive industry, and I would guess at this point in time there are more yoga instructors than fitness instructors.

ACHIEVE LONG-TERM GOALS

To this point we've talked about external forces of change, but it is also important to plan for your internal growth—which is much easier than anticipating unknown changes. The pace at which you grow, the direction you head in, and how far you go are all determined by what you choose as your long-term goals.

Where do you see your business in three, five, or even 10 years? Hopefully, you don't see it as being exactly the same. Even if you work in a service industry, you shouldn't be doing the exact same thing 10 years from now. I'm not saying you will have a new business or career, but changes should take place in what you do and what you offer, as time goes by. With time comes experience, new knowledge, and sometimes changing markets.

This could be the silliest example I use in this book, but think about a rock band. When I was growing up, rock bands went on tour, playing at big stadiums that drew thousands of people. If those same bands today still tried touring those same large venues, they would probably have many empty seats. Those that do still tour are often performing mellower versions of their old tunes and playing in smaller venues that attract an older audience.

That might be the goofiest example I could come up with, but you get the point. And if not, I at least got you feeling nostalgic for a moment.

In the case of your business, think about how you plan to grow and change over the course of time. Most business owners I know would never say that they hope to be doing the same thing in 10 years. Instead, they are usually full of ideas about how they can take what they currently do and enhance it, add to it, change it, and even evolve from it and go to the next, higher step. This is what you need to be thinking about when you put together a long-term plan.

You're probably familiar with the term *S.M.A.R.T. goal.* S.M.A.R.T. stands for specific, measurable, achievable, relevant, and timely. These five adjectives describe what a goal should be in order to be attainable. As a business owner, it is easy to say you have the goal of wanting to "make more money," but this goal is not specific or measurable. Instead of "I want to make more money," say something like "I want to have gross sales of $1,000,000 by the end of my 10th year in business." This goal is specific, measurable, relevant, and timely, as you state the exact time you want to achieve this goal. How achievable it is will depend on how realistic this goal is for you situation.

If you are currently in your fifth year of business and making $500,000 per year, it seems you could achieve doubling your sales within a time frame that doubles how long you've been in business. However, if you're in your eighth year of business and making $250,000, then this goal may not be achievable.

As you look at growing your business, ask yourself *how* you want to grow. What does growth mean to you? Does it refer to growing in sales, profits, or size? Does it mean growing in number of locations, number of clients, and number of markets, or does it simply mean growing in impact within your community? Growth can even refer to a state in which you are satisfied with your business, and just want to sustain it. No matter what growth means to you, you need to be able to define it. Get specific, and make sure you can measure it, and that it is achievable and realistic, is relevant to your business, and has a time frame for completion.

You start by determining a long-term goal you have. I recommend starting with one goal that is most important to you. Once you have determined that goal, the next step is to figure out the action items necessary to achieve it. Usually this involves stating a list of short-term goals that will help you achieve the long-term goal.

Here is an example: Suppose you are a social media expert and your business is teaching others how to excel in the social media world. You teach classes, work with individual clients, and hope to eventually build a full-service marketing firm. Here is a long-term goal you might have, with the breakdown of how to achieve it.

LONG-TERM GOAL: Achieve $500,000 in sales within the next three years.

WHAT IS REQUIRED TO MAKE THAT HAPPEN?

- ❑ Write a book that sells a 1,000 copies at $25 each ($25,000).

- ❑ Increase the number of clients by 33% each year for the next five years (e.g., 25 this year, 33 in year 2, 45 in year 3). (Assume each client is worth $10,000 in revenue. Year 3 would bring in $450,000.)

- ❑ Sell 1 online course for $2,500 each to 10 people ($25,000).

ACTION PLAN—TASKS TO MAKE IT HAPPEN:

- ❑ Join three networks where my most ideal customers will be.
    - Within this group, volunteer to run a seminar.
    - Volunteer to be on the board.

- ❑ Research the best industry-specific conferences and trade shows to attend this year.
    - Attend four as an attendee, and four as a speaker/exhibitor.

- ❑ Partner with other businesses in a cross-marketing campaign.
- ❑ Research ideas for getting free PR.
- ❑ Hire part-time assistant to run PR campaigns/social media.
- ❑ Write a free ebook with CTA.
- ❑ Find a publisher that excels at marketing non-fiction business books.
- ❑ Find a web developer who can help create an online course platform with great UI/UX, or find a platform that already exists, works like a template, and can easily be customized to meet individual needs.

As you can see, you start by setting a goal a few years into the future. However you define *long-term goals* is up to you; I tend to think of them as goals that can be anywhere from three to 10 years out, ideally three to five years. I don't like to go too far out, simply because I don't think it is realistic. Life happens, and a lot can happen over 10 or more years. Most of us who've taken the entrepreneurial path can look back on where we were 10 years ago and never would have imagined where we ended up.

After stating the goal, the next step is to choose specific events that could take place in order to achieve the goal. These events are not only specific, but logically connect to the goal. Stating you want to earn $500,000 in sales, and then determining various ways to get to that number, need to happen in order to make your goal realistic and achievable. A common error is to state the goal, but not back it up with real numbers and practical steps to achieve it. Avoid this by generating several ideas that could realistically work.

Next, look at those events further and determine the action items to ensure the events take place. In the example here, notice the variety of tasks that, when combined, can lead to generating results. This action item list is also very specific. The list can be much longer than what you see here, depending on your goals. The best way to tackle this list is using a brainstorming approach. Write down every idea you can think of that could possibly help you ensure that what needs to happen in order to achieve your goals, can actually happen.

The goal here is not to come up with the best and only ideas, but to generate as many ideas as possible, without overthinking too much. Think of this as a stream-of-consciousness exercise in which you write down everything that comes to mind. Do this for a set amount of time—maybe five or 10 minutes—and then stop writing. Filter through what you wrote to see what jumps out at you as a possible great idea or something worth looking into more.

While this is just one example, when planning for the future growth and success of your business, you should look at setting a few goals. Some will be more important than others; and some may not require much work, while others may require a lot of work. The key is taking the time to *create a plan for your business.* Without a plan, you never know where you'll wind up, and chances are, it won't be the place you really wanted to be.

One final note about defining goals and creating action plans. Every task in your action plan should also have a scheduled time line with deadlines for completing each task. For example, it's good to say you'll join a board as a volunteer, but it's much better to create a list of potential organizations for which you'd like to be a board member and decide that you'll join a board by the end of next month. Your chance of success is greater, the more specific you get.

CHAPTER 12

OVERCOME OBSTACLES

HOPEFULLY THIS BOOK has taught you how to create a plan for success, but there will always be obstacles to overcome along the way. Your business, your personal situation, and other internal and external factors will determine what kind of obstacles you encounter. Some people have unique business ideas with little competition but struggle to build market demand; others work in industries that are so competitive, it's hard to get noticed.

This chapter includes a few common obstacles that business owners experience, with some ideas to help you overcome them.

HIGHLY COMPETITIVE INDUSTRIES

If you provide a service or a product in a highly competitive industry, you probably feel overwhelmed and, at times, question whether or not your business can succeed in a saturated market. You can be successful if you understand one important concept: You must carve out your niche and build your brand upon what makes you different from the crowd.

Think about the example of the lemonade stand (in Chapter 7) and how choosing to focus on selling freshly squeezed organic lemonade with a hint of mint was a way to create a niche in a competitive market. Finding your niche can take some time, but once you go through the exercises in the branding and target market chapters, it should be much easier to discover what makes you different and how you can create unique offerings.

Also note that you don't necessarily have to offer a product or service that no one else offers. The differences come in the presentation, the philosophy, and even the personality of the brand. Everyone has an "it" factor; you just need to figure out what yours is.

If you have a few local competitors, look at their brand and what they offer, and compare it to your brand and what you offer. What is similar and what is different? How do you compare in areas such as skills, personality, vision, experience, network, resources, staff/team, and location? How do your offerings differ? Who do they appeal to?

Once you start asking more detailed questions, you will eventually have an "a-ha" moment and clearly see what makes you unique. It could be that while on the surface you sell the same thing as your competitors, in reality you appeal to completely different markets. The more you can define your brand and offerings in a way that makes you special, the more you can build your marketing around it and get noticed.

Going back to our yoga studios example, remember I said this is a highly competitive industry? It is! So how can each yoga studio create a niche? By recognizing who they appeal to, and building their brand and offerings around those people. Not everyone who practices yoga is the same, and people enjoy it for different reasons.

For me, yoga is about giving myself permission to relax. Restorative or gentle yoga provides this for me. However, I know plenty of people who choose yoga as their preferred workout (whereas for me, that's running). We are two completely different markets. Yoga studios can differentiate themselves by focusing on which market they appeal to—and building their offerings and brand around it.

Don't fear a competitive market. Instead, see the opportunity to discover your niche and provide something unique for your audience.

LIMITED RESOURCES

Most people aren't rich with resources at their disposal when they start a business, so having limited resources is pretty standard. However, for most new business owners, or even those who have been at it for a while, the scenario is one similar to trying to get a job with no experience, but you need a job to get experience. You're trying to build a business that will be profitable, but you can't get profitable without putting money into it. But how do you get money if you need it to get it?

Chapter 10 taught you how to look at what you have and what you don't in order to figure out what you need to get. When resources are limited, such as not having enough money, enough help, or enough skills and knowledge, the best thing you can do is find ways to get ahead that don't require these right away.

For some business owners this could include bartering or trading with others. Perhaps you are a photographer and need a graphic designer but lack the funds. If you know a graphic designer, you could offer to give them a new branding portfolio with new headshots and business branding photos in exchange for graphic design services. I am first and foremost a fan of charging money for your services, but there are certain cases when bartering can be a win/win for both parties.

A word of caution on this: Make sure you iron out all the details before any transaction takes place. You don't want any confusion about who was promised what. Define and agree to the terms of the barter and get it in writing, even if that's just an email.

Another way to handle limited resources is to ask your friends and family to pitch in if they can. This could be with small loans or simply helping out with marketing and social media shares. People who love and support you are usually more than happy to spread the word about your business, and they want to see you succeed.

You can also find a mentor. Many mentors are willing to support an aspiring or new business owner, and to teach them how to build their business and access free resources, and can even connect their mentees with people who might be willing to invest in them. Mentors can teach you about resources you don't even know exist!

There are several non-profit organizations, as well as government organizations, that offer resources, guidance, and education to business owners. The Small Business Administration (SBA) supports local non-profit organizations such as SCORE, which provides mentors for small business owners, as well as workshops, classes, and guidance on business funding. You can search their website (www.sba.gov) for more information and to find a local SCORE chapter.

Finally, collaborate as much as possible. This will allow you to use other people's resources, and they can benefit from what you bring to their audience. It gives you a chance to get out in front of people at very little cost.

FEW QUALITY LEADS

If it makes you feel better, *everyone* has this problem. Remember the example in Chapter 10 of the real estate agent who was sure to tell all of their friends and family about their new business and how this slowly built leads? This is certainly a first step. Make sure everyone you know, knows what you do. Just yesterday at a community event, I bumped into someone I know who was talking to someone else I know. He said to the other person [referring to me], "This is the woman I told you about who does business consulting!" Neither are people I work with, nor are they in my business circles. It made me aware that simply telling someone what I do means they will tell others they know about me, if they meet someone they think could use my services.

Moral of the story: tell everyone who you are and what you do!

Not spending time in the right places also hinders business owners from generating quality leads. You need to be where your leads are. If you're spending too much time in places where your target audience doesn't exist, it's costing you leads. Take time to really strategize and find out where your leads are, and go there. This could be professional organizations, networking groups, companies, industries, social media platforms, conferences, social events, and more.

People like to hang out where they are *comfortable,* rather than exploring new areas. You need to expand into new groups and new places, and build relationships with people outside your immediate circle. Continuously strive to build your network, and you will slowly generate more awareness and more leads.

And finally, follow the steps to qualifying your leads in Chapter 9. Stay laser-focused on your target market, and say no to those who aren't a good fit.

LACK OF SKILLS

As I mentioned earlier, many, if not most, of the business owners I work with had zero business background when they started their business. You don't need a background in finance, entrepreneurship, or any other college major to succeed in business. All you need are a passion for having your own business and the desire to learn how to make it profitable and sustainable. Sounds cliché, but it's spot on.

Being a smart business owner is about continuously learning and about mastering the art of delegating. You should learn as much as possible, and always learn enough to be able to manage those who work for you—but you should also know how to bring in talented people to fill in the gaps. Trust those you hire, and don't micromanage them. Look to them to guide you. Your job isn't to be a tech guru, a finance expert, a CPA, or an MBA. Your job is to run your machine. You hire tech gurus, you hire finance experts, you hire CPAs, and you hire business experts to work *for you.*

Don't get discouraged if you feel underqualified, not experienced enough, or not educated enough. There is a path in front of you full of opportunities to learn, collaborate, and hire talent. It's up to you to create the path and lead the way.

FINAL THOUGHTS

My hope is that this book has addressed the primary and necessary components of creating and building a business that will be profitable, be sustainable, and continue to grow for years to come. While trends will come and go, technology and social media will change, and there will always be new products and services on the market, while others fall away, the emphasis in this book focuses on foundational principles that won't be so transient.

Listening to your customers, solving problems, being fiscally responsible, understanding your profitability and your numbers, selling with empathy, being resourceful, and creating products and services that others want and need, will never go out of style. Use this book not only as a learning tool, but as a foundation to always return to as your market changes, technology changes, and competition rises, and you need to adjust successfully and grow with these changes.

As you continue to move forward in your business journey, no matter how long you are in business, you are always learning. That's what keeps the entrepreneurial life so exciting! It's a constant experiment: trying out different approaches and strategies, and seeing what works and what doesn't. My goal with this book is to give you reliable strategies based on education and experience that will teach you better ways to manage your growth, learn from your mistakes, and recognize opportunities.

Finally, let your passion guide you—a passion not only for your business, but for the life you wish to lead. At the heart of every entrepreneur is a desire to live the life you choose. I hope this book has given you the tools you need to create that life.

APPENDIX: STRATEGIC PLAN TEMPLATE

OVERVIEW

Create a plan to assess the current state of your business; decide where you want the business to go (your vision and goals) and why you want to achieve this vision (your mission); and determine what is needed to get it there (your objectives, action items, and resources), and when you can conceivably achieve it (time frame). Review your plan every three to six months or so to make sure you are on track to achieve your goals, or assess if something needs to change.

STEP 1: BUSINESS OVERVIEW

1. Describe your business in two to three sentences.

STEP 2: DETERMINE CURRENT STATE (Assessment)

1. Describe the current state of your business. This would include current sales, customers, market conditions, financial stability, staffing, marketing, and overall operations.

2. Analyze your competition. Who are your current competitors, how do they impact your business, how are you similar, and how are you different from them?

3. What are the current state and trends of the industry? Is there demand or need for what you offer?

4. What are your business's current strengths? Weaknesses? (This refers to internal strengths and weaknesses.)

5. What potential opportunities are there for your business? This could include growing demand for your products/services, changes in your industry, reduced competition, or availability of new technology.

6. What external threats exist? This could include negative economic conditions, increased competition, or changes in market demand.

STEP 3: WHERE YOU WANT YOUR BUSINESS TO GO
(Vision and Goals)

1. Describe the long-term vision for your business. Where do you want your business to be in the future?

2. List the goals for your business. This can include goals for growth, customers, sales, operations, and finance.

STEP 4: WHY YOU WANT TO ACHIEVE THIS VISION
(Mission)

1. What is your business's mission? What is the why behind your vision and goals you stated in Step 3?

STEP 5: WHAT IS NEEDED TO GET YOU THERE
(Objectives, Action Items, and Resources)

1. Create a list of your objectives. What do you expect to accomplish over the course of the next weeks and months to help you achieve your goals? For example, suppose your goal is to increase your revenue by $120,000 over the next year. Your objectives might be to increase your revenue each month by $10,000 dollars.

2. Create a list of action items to meet your objectives. Each objective should have its own list of action items. Using the previous example, if your objective is to increase revenue by $10,000 each month, create an action item list for how you can accomplish that. How many more clients/customers do you need to acquire to increase revenue by $10,000 per month, and what steps will you take to acquire them?

3. Create a list of resources you will need to achieve your goals. Do you need additional funds? To hire new employees or independent contractors? New space for the location of your business? New partnerships for projects? New skills to acquire? Think of various resources you need to make things happen, and create a list of ideas on how you will acquire them.

STEP 6: WHEN CAN YOU ACHIEVE IT (Time Frame)

1. Your goals, objectives, and action plan should all have time frames associated with them. Give each goal a deadline. Each objective a scheduled time frame, and each action item a specific date range to implement.

   For example, your goal is to increase revenue by $120,000 by December 31st of the upcoming year, your objective is to increase revenue by $10,000 each month over the course of that year, and your action items are to: 1) Contact current customers to upsell them on services (week one), 2) Create a new social media marketing plan highlighting CTA e-book, which leads to an invite to purchase your 1-year service package (week two), 3) Sponsor a local event that generates 50,000 attendees, whom you can add to your email list (week three), and 4) Email your professional network asking for referrals, and offering to reciprocate (week four).

STEP 7: REVIEW AND RE-EVALUATE

1. As time progresses, and you get different and sometimes unexpected results from implementing your plan, it is necessary to continuously evaluate and re-evaluate your plan to ensure it is effective and generating the results you desire. Make changes as needed along the way.

To download this template, as well as other business planning templates, please visit kdawsonco.com/resources.

ABOUT THE AUTHOR

Kim is a no-nonsense business strategist specializing in helping small business owners and entrepreneurs connect their ambition to the results they desire. She specializes in revenue generation, pricing, scalability, business development, business growth, and branding.

Kim started her journey in entrepreneurship as a child, creating marketing materials and sales processes for the art creations she sold door-to-door in her neighborhood. Her entrepreneurial spirit remained through college and beyond, with Kim working in numerous business models and industries. She was co-founder of a bootstrapped software startup that taught her how to start with nothing and take big risks to grow (and eventually sell) a successful company, and she owned a health and fitness business, including a brick and mortar studio.

Aside from her entrepreneurial journey, Kim has worked in a wide range of industries, from technology to health to manufacturing to retail to service. That gives her a unique perspective on marketing, finances, business growth, and how businesses run.

Now as a business strategist, Kim helps her clients grow their businesses so they have more money and more time, and create a bigger impact on the world. She lives in Massachusetts with her two children and regularly travels to her hometown on Long Island, New York. She loves to cook, explore the outdoors, run, hike, practice photography, and listen to live jazz. She's also host of The Sassy Strategist podcast, where she shares business wisdom and interviews other successful business owners with a passion for sharing their own stories, successes, and lessons.

Made in United States
North Haven, CT
26 August 2022